WITH OUR OWN FOUR HANDS

AND A LOT OF HELP FROM OUR FRIENDS AND NEW NEIGHBORS SWAIN SKI AREA CAME TO BE

by

Dave and Bina Robinson

authorHOUSE

AuthorHouse™
1663 Liberty Drive, Suite 200
Bloomington, IN 47403
www.authorhouse.com
Phone: 1-800-839-8640

© 2007 Dave and Bina Robinson. All rights reserved.

No part of this book may be reproduced, stored in a retrieval system, or transmitted by any means without the written permission of the author.

First published by AuthorHouse 11/16/2007

ISBN: 978-1-4343-4041-2 (sc)

Library of Congress Control Number: 2007908253

Printed in the United States of America
Bloomington, Indiana

This book is printed on acid-free paper.

Contents

Foreword	vii
Acknowledgements	ix
Dave's Chronicle	1
The Way I Remember It	13
Trail and Slope Development	51
Tows and Lifts	59
Snowmaking	67
Base Lodge	77
The Cafeteria Crew	85
The Swain Ski Patrol	97
Swain Ski School	103
The Swain Ski Shop and Rental Department	109
Money	141
Ski area's effect on the hamlet of Swain	151
My Chapter	173
Growing up on the Ski Slopes	183
Andy's Recollections	191
Janet's Recollections	201
Potpourri	205
Appendix	215
Index	221
About the Authors	231

Foreword

What began as Swain Ski Slopes, later called Swain Ski Center, then Swain Ski and Snowboard Center, and now, just this year, Swain Winter Resort, actually began in Philadelphia during World War II. It was the brainchild of my late husband, David Dunlop Robinson, conceived at a time when the freedom to conduct our new life together was curtailed by the World War II. We considered ourselves very fortunate because, when he wasn't at sea, Dave was working for the Army Transport Service on a derrick barge in the Port of Philadelphia loading heavy equipment for the troops in Europe. The work was dangerous and went on seven nights a week, many of them 18 and 20 hours long, but we got to see each other most days. I was working the graveyard shift as a machine shop inspector at the General Electric Company. We knew we were fortunate being together at least some of the time but needed something to look forward to after the war was over when we would be released from an existence not of our choosing. I was the skier, but it was Dave who came up with the idea of developing a ski area for western New York.

In the last few years, I have become ever more acutely aware that I am the only one left with the knowledge of how the hamlet of Swain became a ski resort. Since it is no longer possible for us to work on this book together, it will start with an account Dave wrote several years ago followed by some of the details as I remember them. (Thanks to Nick Schiavetti of the Swain Ski Patrol for finding Dave's account on his computer and forwarding it to mine.) It is a pity that Dave is not here to contribute his wonderful sense of humor, which doesn't show up in his matter-of- fact account (but survives in the children's chapters), as well as his knowledge of outdoor developments with which I became less closely associated as the area expanded.

With no records to work from and chronological sense not being my strong suit, I shall be following a stream of consciousness rather than a more conventional time-line format to give readers a more detailed idea of how the hamlet of Swain in the northeastern corner of New York's Allegany County became a ski resort. These somewhat random recollections will be followed by several short chapters on specific aspects of the area's development and its effect on the hamlet of Swain.

Acknowledgements

I am uncomfortably aware that I am unable to remember all the events and the names of all the people who have made significant contributions to the development of Swain Ski Center and beg their forgiveness. In the interests of local history and the history of the sport of skiing, it seems best to set down what comes to mind, the alternative being not to write at all in which case what knowledge I can contribute would become unavailable when I "shuffle off this mortal coil."

First, thanks to the late Barbara Swain, Dorothy Kendall, and my sister Elizabeth Aitchison Bruggeman who urged me to get on with it; Town of Grove Historian, Marilyn Yencer Weidman, who helped reconstruct the past; Irene Szabo, president of the Finger Lakes Trail Association for the early railroad information; Harry and Lyle Weaver who told me a lot of things I had forgotten or hadn't known about; Nick Schiavetti, Harry Stoneham, and Herb Lehman of the Swain Ski Patrol; Joan and Chic Carlucci for ski school information; PhotoShop expert Rob Huffman for colorizing the cover photo; son-in-law Jim Pownall for his computer expertise and limitless supply of patience; and, last but not least, our children, Challice, Jeanie, Andy and Janet for reading this manuscript and contributing their perspectives to say nothing of their voluntary and involuntary childhood contributions.

Dave's Chronicle

It was my intention to make no changes to Dave's 1992 account, but I have yielded to our children's wishes that some of their recollections be included. Any additions are footnoted. —Bina

How Did The Robinsons Happen To Locate A Ski Area At Swain?

David Dunlop Robinson

I have been urged a lot lately (say in the last three years) to record how we started the Swain Ski Area. Friend and next door neighbor now in Arizona, Barb Swain has been after us for what it would mean someday to her son and to our grandchildren. And the all-volunteer Swain Ski Patrol, one of the oldest continually operating chapters of the National Ski Patrol in the country, has been after us for information about their origins.

Why A Ski Area At All?

As with many things, personal background was responsible.

Bina was raised in Pittsfield, Mass. within walking distance (for her) of Bousquet's Ski Center, one of the early ones in the USA. She was an accomplished and enthusiastic skier by the time she came to the University of Rochester, which was unusual then. I was more or less brought up at Aunt Nell's cottage in Vine Valley on Canandaigua Lake, and my goal while in college was to spend Summers At The Lake at Aunt Nell's cottage, which meant either working near there, or working at a job that gave summers off. Teaching did not appeal at that time because of low pay. We did not meet until my senior year (Bina's junior year) at the University of Rochester. We both had cubicles in the stacks in the U of R library, but it was not until Mike Klein and I ascended the stairs one day early in our senior year, and saw Bina trying to change the lighting arrangement in her cubicle, that we met. She lacked a part, which I brought the next day.[1] Had Mike asked her to go out with him before I did, I would not have asked her, and there would be no Swain Ski Center today.

Following graduation from the U of R, I went into the Marines on June 10, 1943. Standing in front of me in all formations of our platoon on Parris Island was Charles Schobinger of Chicago, who I believe later became head of the National Ski Patrol system for the USA. I don't recall talking to him.

I was discharged from the Marines for a training injury that September. Over the following Christmas holidays I joined the Merchant Marine and, was sent to Sheepshead Bay on Long Island for training. In April 1944 I was assigned to Pier 98 in Philadelphia as a deck hand, later

---

[1] Jeanie: "We as children loved hearing this story. The part Mother needed was an adapter; Dad told her they had a whole attic full at home, got an advance on his dollar a week allowance, bought one at a hardware store, and installed it the next day"

Mate, on a derrick barge loading tanks, locomotives, etc. into ships. This gave us the opportunity to get married, which we did on May 14, 1944, the day Bina graduated from college.

I was stationed in Philadelphia for a year. During that time we discussed what we would do after the war. We wanted to work for ourselves, but did not have any clear idea of what kind of work.

Our first fumbling idea of a job that in our innocence we thought would give us summers off, was to build dormitories for the large numbers of New Yorkers who came up on ski trains to ski at Bousquet's in Pittsfield. But after the Philadelphia job ended, and I was shipping on tankers and was between ships in Boston in the summer of 1945, I looked up an acquaintance there. It happened that he planned to go into building, and showed me drawings he had made for some sort of group housing he hoped to construct when the war was over. I realized then that building dormitories would be a far more expensive project than I could afford, and required technical skills I did not have. Nothing at that time, U of R or working summers at Kodak, fitted me for that. We dropped the idea.

Later, while on bow watch at night on a tanker, the idea struck me that Rochester had no ski area but had a lot of snow, so we should look for a hill, buy it, and put up a rope tow, which I had heard Bina describe. (Actually there were several small ski areas, and a big one for those days, Bill De Wolfe's Burby Hollow in the northern part of the Bristol Hills, but we didn't know it. Bill, a veteran of the 10th Mountain Division, later ran our ski school for ten years.)

So that is one scenario for getting the idea of starting a ski area. The only trouble with it is that Gordy Kester (a college classmate) tells me that he remembers my talking in college, and this was before my senior year when I met Bina, about starting a ski area. And this rings a bell too. At one time, and it may have been then, I had the idea of using the logging roads on South Hill above the Ottley farm in Vine Valley on Canandaigua Lake as ski trails, and shepherding groups of skiers down them, stopping at the farm, where Mrs. Ottley would feed us.

Why At Swain?

Bina and I took a leave of mine, a couple of weeks in the winter of 1946, to spend at Aunt Nell's cottage in Vine Valley to look for a hill to buy. I had done very little skiing before starting the ski area, and none at that point, but Bina knew what was required in the way of skiable pitches for all classes of skier

We were so green that we did not know when we started looking that more snow collects on an east-facing slope, and that most snow for Western NYS comes from Lake Erie, except for a good snowbelt for a few miles south of Lake Ontario, and some snow from coastal storms that comes inland. Most Lake Ontario snow in Western NYS melts rapidly, being near the lake. The Lake Erie snow, falling inland on higher ground, lasts longer.[2] As far as locating a hill goes, that two weeks was largely a waste of time. We did learn that South Hill has less snow than the Bristol Hills, and the Bristol Hills did not have enough. This was before snowmaking.

---

[2] Dave was writing about central western New York rather than central New York where one of the best snow belts occurs east of Lake Ontario.

Following that, we used a more systematic approach. We bought contour maps of all the area for 60 miles to the east, south and west of Rochester and marked likely looking east slopes and visited them when practical, on leaves when I was still shipping out, and on weekends, holidays and evenings when I was working for Eastman Kodak in Rochester after my discharge in the summer of 1946. During the winter we learned how much more snow there is around Warsaw than most places that would be practical to reach from Rochester, given the roads at that time. We talked to the owners of many parcels of land around Western NYS, and tried to buy several. It was good experience. I learned that to buy farmland you had to be a good listener, and count your time as worth nothing. The farmers were not going to sell to someone they did not know. You had to give them enough time to feel they knew you. We kept widening the circle from Rochester, and did not overlook anything that looked possible on the contour maps.

It was on one such excursion, this one in the winter of 1947, that we drove past Swain on Route 408-A, now Route 70. Looking at the hill, I remarked that it looked good, but we knew that a north-facing hill would not receive as much snow as one facing east. Bina said, "I don't care. It looks more like a ski area than any other place we have looked at." We turned the car around and drove thru Swain, parking about where the town highway department sheds are now, and walked uphill, across the top of what is now the Novice Area and into what is now Middle Brewer Slope, following a logging road that can still be partially traced thru the woods. There was a lot of snow. So we withdrew the requirement that the hill must face east, but kept looking all around Western NYS.

As it happens there is a peculiarity about the Swain Hill that we did not realize at the time, but local pilots later told us that they observed that if it was snowing any place around, it would be snowing there. One assumed there was an updraft that caused the clouds to drop their snow there. I noticed in later years that I'd leave Swain with snow falling. It would stop before I reached Canaseraga. The sun would be shining in Hornell during the two or three hours I'd be there having a part machined, then upon return the snowfall would start a half mile west of Canaseraga, and when I reached Swain it would have been snowing the entire time I was in Hornell, not a lot, two or three inches, but those falls, daily during some periods, do more good than the big ones that usually seem to be followed by a thaw.

Finally we settled on Swain as the place for a ski area. Somebody told us that to do anything there we had to see Fred Blakley who "ran" Swain. I remember driving into Swain on a warm Saturday morning in the spring of 1947 and stopping the car to speak to a group of men standing and sitting on the concrete steps in front of what had obviously once been a store (now Maude's Country Store). I put my head out the window and asked "Where can I find Fred Blakley?" A stocky man sitting on the steps, wearing a white Stetson, said "He's gone fishing." But he walked over and introduced himself. He was Fred Blakley, timber and land buyer, snow fence manufacturer and saw mill owner.

There are several people whose help was vital in the early days at Swain. We could not have survived without the unpaid help of Fred Blakley (and Dick Clark who worked in Kodak in the same division I did).

Fred identified the owners of the land we wanted, Erma Gleason Babcock and John Brewer. Each had a "farm" of 20 acres and eventually agreed to sell the land to us, retaining their houses,

The first of 15 or 20 such land purchases over the years, Erma's land included a barn which is still part of the Base Lodge complex. We paid $400 for each piece of land, $100 down and the balance at 6% spread over several years. A small part of the barn became the first "Warming Hut."

The land purchase made a hole in our assets -$1,600 saved during the war. We also had a Jeep Station Wagon and a few clothes. We rented a two room furnished apartment on Kenilworth Terrace behind the Dental Dispensary. I was working shifts at Kodak in the dark rooms for about a dollar an hour, the only job I was able to find that would give me weekends off to run a ski area when we finally started one. Bina obtained a job teaching Phys. Ed. at Brockport Central School which paid quite a bit more.[3]

Despite the kind of difficulties you can imagine, we did manage, with hand tools, to clear a slope, called "Main Slope" in those days, and install a rope tow. Without a replacement motor which Fred Blakley loaned us, and later financed, we would not have completed the first weekend. There weren't many weekends of skiing in that or the next few years, but we continued to expand. Our rent for the first apartment, the next one on Pierpont Street, and later a small house on Calkins Road cost us $10 a week, a sum that let us continue to put money into Swain. I remember trying at one point to live from Sunday night to Friday

---

[3] Actually the salary was $2000 a year and required Greyhound bus fare to get there.

noon on $25 a week, exclusive of rent, and even we couldn't do it. In theory it was enough, but there was always something, a new tire, etc. For ten years Bina and I ran the ski slopes working weekends, holidays and vacations at Swain while I worked for 40 hours a week at Kodak. The ski area was open only on weekends and school holidays in winter at that time. And, of course, only when there was enough natural snow to run. Bina left the Brockport job to teach at The Harley School in Brighton.

And there is no way we could have kept the ski area going without the volunteer help of Dick Clark and his family, and dozens of other people, in the early years. Dick could do so many things I couldn't at that time, such as carpentry and wiring, and he was very good at hooking up things and making them work. During the fall of 1947 before the area opened, we three attended first aid classes in East High, and Bina, Dick and I constituted the first Swain Ski Patrol. Later Dick's boys, David and Bill, were on the patrol. Bill still lives in the region in Honeoye Falls. Dick died of a heart attack in January 1958 following trail sweep on the first day the first T-Bar ran. It was Dick Tardiff's idea that we rename Main Slope "Clark Slope," and he built the memorial toboggan shelter-sitting bench that for years was situated in the opening at the top of Clark Slope. (I don't know what happened to the bronze plaque honoring Dick.) Mary Clark's running the cafeteria for ten years also helped greatly.

In retrospect, it is remarkable that the ski area ever survived. During our 30 year stay there it was always a shoestring operation. We ran it weekends for the first ten years while I worked at Kodak. Bina was able to quit her job at Harley School, and would drive down to Swain on Wednesday mornings, and I'd take the bus to Mt. Morris on Friday evenings, where Bina would pick me up. I had progressed well at Kodak, and several times we almost gave up the ski slopes.

For the second ten years we still ran Swain without snowmaking, lived there full time, brought up four children, and had no outside income. It is difficult now to see how we managed, but we were both of Scottish extraction, penny pinchers, and could Make It Do, Use It Up, and Go Without. It was a very low overhead operation. We could survive financially on six weekends of skiing. If there were 12 weekends, we'd make money in a tax sense. One year there were 16 weekends.

I know of only one other group of ski area operators, the old Ellicottville Ski Club (who later started Holiday Valley) who went around stealing ideas. It is important to attend every ski area operators' conference that you can attend cheaply. But it is also important to get out in the field and see what works, and doesn't work, at other areas. I did this when I was still working at Kodak and for 20 years afterward. Every spring I used to go on an idea stealing trip to New England and talk to anybody who would stand still. The only people that I know of who ever came to me to steal ideas were the Ellicottville group, and they got a beauty that I stole from Ed Taylor in the Adirondacks. It applied to a cheap way to build a rope tow, not of much use today.

Weekend operation with pick-up crews was very nice from our standpoint. We'd use Fred Blakley's woods crew to run the lifts, and during the second ten years, after Mary Clark left, Bina would employ area women in the cafeteria. Sometimes I'd have one or two men to help outdoors creating new ski trails and installing T Bars in the spring, summer and fall, and sometimes not. One year when we didn't have any money I redid the interior of the Ski Barn, as the Base Lodge became known, alone. Half way thru the job you could stand in the basement and look up past two floors I had removed to the rafters. Alone I put in the main steel support beam. I don't really see now how I did it. The posts supporting it were easy, of course. I put in two new floors that badly needed doing to handle the crowds we were getting on occasion.

Snowmaking, which we tackled for the third time in 1968, created an entirely different ski area (one not nearly so much fun to run) but we did for our third ten years at Swain, but that is another story, and probably not such an interesting one.

Snowmaking is so expensive that the weekends-only operation had to come to an end. Low overhead changed to high overhead, and eventually seven days and seven nights of skiing a week. It meant permanent crews winter and summer. It gives enjoyment to many more people, employs more, brings a lot more money into the local economy, but as a return on investment the pre-snowmaking operation might have been better, as the investment was so much smaller. But with all competitors using machine-made snow, we had to too. Unlike our first two snow-making machines, this one, entirely homemade, worked very well, thanks largely to Bill Jenkins, a successful Warsaw farmer, and cooperation from the Kissing Bridge Ski Center. The good thing about snowmaking is that you knew you were going to run.

And shining throughout most of the thirty years was The Bank of Castile. Sometime during our first ten years, and I think it was to buy the Riley Ulster land which was necessary to run Main Slope (now Clark Slope) directly to the bottom of the hill (The house later became the first ski patrol building.) we borrowed money from Bud VanArsdale at the bank, a happy relationship that extended throughout our stay at Swain. There were a lot of financially hard times, but I always went out of the bank feeling better than when I went in. I am afraid that in today's climate of merger and acquisition, few banks have the patience and understanding to nurture small businesses, and we were very small. I understand that during Robin Smith's tenure at Swain, the ski area became that bank's largest single customer.

In ski area operation then it was almost axiomatic that you should do the opposite of whatever the national press (except Don Metivier) recommended, and Cut Your Coat to Fit Your Cloth. The number of bankrupt ski area owners I have talked to who said, "But all the ski magazines said that a ski area has to . . . . " Reporters don't pay the bills. They are paid for writing a story, and unfortunately some of them felt they had to say something. At one point a ski reporter quoted me completely inaccurately, and when I protested said, "I know you didn't say that, but wasn't it a good story!" Which seems to be what counted, not accuracy. We received a lot of cooperation from local reporters.

I figure that I have made every mistake it is possible to make except spending too much money, which is probably the greatest mistake of all. Obviously we did some things right.

We did not attain the goal of "Summers At The Lake" until after we retired from Swain. And oddly enough, had I remained at Kodak, we would have had Summers At The Lake, or large parts of the summers, several decades before we did, and I certainly would have earned more money during my working life, and would have retired with a good pension. Leaving the remarkable security of the Kodak of that period, and a gorgeous house, was a very difficult thing to do with four pre-school children, and there were certainly times when I wished that we were back in that well-ordered life.

Yet, had we been able to foresee that we would work for the first 20 years without any time off pursuing the ski area goal, and for less financial reward during our 30 year working lives, we would still have done it.

One time in the early days at Swain when I was shoveling snow on the tow path, a young man riding up shouted to me, "I'm sure glad there are guys like you who want to run ski areas so that guys like me can ski."

Dave Robinson 17 March 1992
1920-2001

The Way I Remember It

Bina Aitchison Robinson

The following stream of consciousness account consists of recollections as they occurred to me. It would have been a lot more comprehensive if Dave and I could have worked on it together. Since that is no longer possible, I have done the best I could to present the facts as a record of local history as well as for the entertainment and edification of skiers and budding entrepreneurs everywhere. Subsequent chapters will deal with more specific aspects of the area's development and its effects on the little hamlet of Swain.

It all began over 60 years ago, in 1944 to be exact, on the second floor of a modest Philadelphia brick row house. In order to help with the war effort, Ethel McHenry, a busy practicing nurse, offered to rent the second of the three stories that comprised her childhood home to a service couple. Dave was lucky enough to get there first and secure it for our first home together. It consisted of a decent-sized furnished bedroom, a much smaller back room, which we used as an office, and the luxury of our own bathroom off the stair landing. We were also privileged to share the kitchen.

Dave and Bina Robinson

We were married on my graduation day from the University of Rochester and took a train to Philadelphia that same night sharing a car with the inebriated members of a bowling team who used the aisle for a bowling lane. It was far from an ideal wedding trip but we felt very fortunate that we could be together and thankful that we could even share a seat. People often had to stand or sit on their suitcases for long journeys in those wartime days when more civilians, to say nothing of thousands of servicemen, were traveling on trains because gasoline was rationed.

Ethel was a good scout and an ideal landlady who became a good friend as well. In spite of the fact that she suffered from tic douloureux (a painful facial neuralgia), she worked long shifts at a hospital where she took most of her meals. This left the first floor kitchen mostly in my inexperienced hands. I knew enough to empty the drip pan under the ice box but precious little about cooking which consisted mainly of reheating the contents of cans and making sandwiches for Dave to take to work when he was working on the docks.

I'd never seen cockroaches before, but didn't consider them a problem because they only came out at night and skittered out of sight as soon as I turned on the light. It wasn't that the kitchen was unclean, just that the beasties had had a couple of centuries to get established in that row of adjoined houses.

The house was like a brick oven in summer and brick icebox in winter. I can still see Alfred, the elderly "houseman" who tended the furnaces of a number of houses in the neighborhood, shaking his head and saying, "There ain't nobody but me understands this old furnace." It was soon apparent that even Alfred didn't understand it too well or maybe it was just too old and worn out to function properly. I had a few goes at trying to make it work myself but was never successful. It was easier just to stay in bed wearing mittens to keep my hands warm while holding up a book. Trolley cars rumbled by on nearby 22nd Street loudly enough to interrupt ordinary conversation, but they gave us transportation almost to the door.

As the need for war materials ebbed, the Army Transport Service operation was curtailed sending Dave to sea for the following year. General Electric discontinued its third shift around the same time. I took a job teaching history at South Philadelphia High School for Girls to fill in for someone on maternity leave. At the end of the school year, I returned to my family in Pittsfield and took another job with General Electric, this time as an engineering assistant on a pilot production project,[4] until Dave was finally "home from the sea" and had settled on a job with Eastman Kodak in Rochester working in a darkroom developing customers' film. Being history majors with mere B.A.s did not qualify us for many jobs especially at the time when servicemen were returning to resume their old positions.

After the war was over, Dave rented a two-room furnished apartment in Rochester where I joined him. Our second home had a small kitchen but involved a shared bathroom down the hall. The icebox was an improvement, however, because it was mounted on the wall over the

---

[4] The purpose of this project was to improve the efficiency of manufacturing a capacitor used in fluorescent lights before a new plant for its manufacture was built along the Hudson River at Fort Edward, New York. Pyranol, the viscous liquid dielectric used in these capacitors, was later found in large quantities in the Hudson River causing one of the country's worst toxic waste spills. That was back in the 1940's, but General Electric has only recently acknowledged the problem. My exposure was minimal because it involved only the test units we assembled in the lab. I have often wondered, however, how the vapor rising from the big treatment tanks might have affected the men and women who inhaled the vapor rising from the tanks for eight hours a day.

sink so the melt water automatically dripped down the sink drain. This apartment was smaller but more comfortable than our wartime abode and had a bright southern exposure.

We were apartment Number 10, which meant our guests had to ring the doorbell downstairs 10 times to get our attention. The bell being at the far end of the house made it difficult to hear let alone keep track of the rings. We solved that one by mounting a bell on a bureau (our own, not the landlady's) inside a window and dropping a cord to a little-used passage along the side of the house.

The gate-leg dining table became our next office. It would be another 20 years or so before we were to graduate from dining tables to a real office outfitted with two used desks and file cabinets and a couple of already antique Underwood typewriters.

Mrs. Haller was a conscientious landlady who ran the house well from a practical standpoint and provided homes for 12 people, but she did so with an insensitivity that sometimes caused us to refer to her as Mrs. Heller.

My recollection about our financial state is even more dismal than Dave's. In Philadelphia we managed our finances by putting the cash from our pay envelopes in the pocket of a seldom-used coat. Whenever one of us needed money, we would just take out another $5 or $10 bill. Either was good for a lot of groceries and street car rides. Because we only took what we needed, paying the rent was no problem and if we occasionally ran short before payday, we were able to glean enough by going through my pockets for leftover change.

Mostly, the money just accumulated, however. Whenever it became more than we could foresee using, it was deposited in a savings account. Dave must have handled this for the most part because I can only vaguely recall going to a bank there except for the fact it had an attractive tiled floor. My recollection is that I left Philadelphia while Dave was still at sea with a little less than $3,000.

After joining Dave, I took a job teaching physical education at Brockport Central School, about a 20-mile Greyhound bus ride from downtown Rochester. I was not really qualified, but women PE teachers were in short supply so we made do with each other. They were a nice bunch of kids and I enjoyed working with them.

We chose Rochester because there were no local ski areas as far as we knew whereas Bousquet's was already well established within the broad city limits of Pittsfield, and larger areas in Vermont were within an easy day's drive. Except for a very short rope tow at Powdermill Park in Pittsford, Rochester skiers had to drive to Old Forge or Snow Ridge in the Adirondacks in order to ride up before skiing down. We later learned that Bill DeWolfe, a 10th Mountain Division veteran, had started a private ski club in Burby Hollow in the Bristol Hills south of Rochester. Rochester school teacher Henry DiClemente was later to start another private area farther north in the same valley so we weren't the only ones who felt western New York skiers needed a place to ride up and ski down. The Ellicottville Ski Club farther west also had its own rope tow, an operation that was later moved out of town to become Holiday Valley.

Dave and Bina Robinson

Thanks to the generosity of Dave's parents, Alice Mae (Challice) and Ray McLeod Robinson, who kindly loaned us their car, we spent weekends and holidays looking at hills in ever widening semi-circles south of Rochester. As our search expanded, we realized how much territory was involved and invested almost the entire amount of our savings in a very low-powered Willys Jeep station wagon. The low power was an unwelcome factor because hills of any size or steepness had to be climbed in the second of its three forward gears. Its light weight and far-from-aerodynamic structure made it tricky to handle on windy, ice-covered roads, but it got us where we needed to go. Besides, not much else was available right after the war. I think it cost $2,200, the major part of our savings. Shortly after that, thanks to Dave's good instruction, I acquired my first driver's license.

Every day we didn't have to work at our regular jobs was spent driving around looking for a place for our ski-area-to-be. Failing to find anything close to Rochester, we started looking at the steep hills around the southern end of Canandaigua Lake only to learn, as Dave describes in his account, that the snowfall in that area was too sparse.

I vividly remember staying in Aunt Nell's summer cottage on Canandaigua Lake one cold winter fortnight. The very heavy living room rug billowed up and down like a magic carpet at the whim of the winds that swept under the floor from across the mile-wide lake. We almost had to put our feet in the fireplace to feel any warmth and the bedroom would have qualified for a frozen food locker. It might have been better if we had used Dave's room upstairs but we, perhaps unwisely, opted for the downstairs guest room with windows on three sides. Dave distinguished himself by making a run across the long living room to the kitchen every morning and lighting the three lantern-like kerosene burners on the kitchen stove. The kitchen was also exposed to the elements on three sides, a delight in summer, but darned drafty in the winter. After waiting a few minutes for the upper air to warm up a bit, we both grabbed our clothes, made a dash for the kitchen, where we dressed standing on the wooden chairs to take advantage of the warmer air higher up.

After breakfast, we'd set off to investigate new territory, assessing possible slopes from the car and walking over the likeliest ones. At dusk, we'd return to start a fire in the fireplace and chop away some ice near the shore to get a couple of buckets of water. In those days before the current obsession with motor boats, the lake water was probably purer than that of many municipal water supplies. All this activity would probably have been considered part of the fun by a group on a winter camping trip. For us, it was just another uncomfortable factor to be dealt with. The problem with the lack of snow as we realized later was a matter of elevation. Even though the hills were higher than those around Swain, generally by c. 1,000 feet, their height was made possible by the fact that the valleys were lower. In effect, the hills around Swain were at the same altitude as the upper half of those around the southern end of Canandaigua Lake.

As I recall it, the first time we saw what was to become our ski area, we were just driving past Swain on the way to look at other possible sites we had identified on our contour maps. The map encompassing Swain correctly showed the lower east slopes as being too close to vertical as is typical of glaciated valleys, but the less heavily wooded northeast nose caught our attention. It was then that I had what seemed to be a vision. I recall saying, "I can just see a T-bar running up there."

It was a vision at least in the sense that is exactly where our first T-bar was installed. Over half a century later, however, I can't honestly claim that I actually visualized anything that wasn't actually there. A T-bar was too far beyond our means to waste time even thinking about at that time. I mention this because of the prophetic manner in which the site seemed to present itself to us. In spite of the fact that it faced northeast (actually all the way from due east to due north) we added it to the list of sites we would be checking for snowfall.

In those days, long before snow-making became an option, natural snowfall was everything, Although more snow fell farther west closer to Lake Erie, Swain seemed to offer the best combination of snow cover and skiing terrain near Rochester, our anticipated market.

The wooded slopes rose out of the back yards of the little hamlet's houses, notably those of Erma Gleason Babcock and John Brewer, whose adjacent lots ran all the way to the top of the hill or nearly so. We would later acquire terrain at the top and farther east from Fred's brother, Ben Blakley.

Fortunately for us, the land was of little value, having been carelessly timbered off in the previous century leaving a thin layer of soil over clay and shale bedrock. Also fortunately for us, Erma's father, Mark Heath, had some 20 or 30 years earlier cleared and plowed the gentler section in the middle of the hill that had first caught our attention. This meant that the timber growth, although still substantial, was lighter here than elsewhere.

The lower third of John's land was mostly cleared, probably for pasture as it would have been too steep for plowing. I can remember Bill Whitney, whose farm was atop the hill across the narrow valley carved by Ewart Creek, mowing it for us with his team of horses, one white, the other black. I wish we had taken photographs at the time, but it didn't occur to us how helpful they would be in reconstructing the past or that we would ever be writing an account of it. All our attention was focused on getting the area started.

Erma was a prime example of the graciousness and refinement we recognized in members of the older generation in the area. She and John were both agreeable to reducing their tax burden by unloading land they were not using. John was once overheard to remark to somebody that if he was going to buy land, he'd buy enough to stand up on. As I recall the transaction, we paid them each $10 a month year round until the purchase price and interest had been met. This went on for several years before the debt was erased and we actually owned the land we were using.

I can remember feeling sorry when we had to tell John, who hadn't kept track, when we made the next to last payment. He trusted us and didn't question it. I can also remember John, who was well on in years, in his 80's perhaps, and with just one eye to see with, accompanying us on foot all the way to the top of the hill to show us the fallen remains of a grove of American chestnut trees that had been destroyed by the widespread blight that obliterated this species just as white ash trees, another useful species, are now being threatened by another blight.

In spite of his limited eyesight, John was surprisingly agile at negotiating thick second growth forest and climbing over the fallen chestnut tree limbs. We were later told that back when he was a member of a timber-cutting crew, he had been very agile, "like a monkey" in the woods.[5]

Once we had the use of the land, the real work began. We set ourselves the task of clearing enough of it to open the following winter. You could still make out the plow ridges, but just barely, on the less heavily wooded middle section of the hill on Erma's land that had originally caught our attention. The subsequent growth of trees and brush was lighter here than elsewhere so it was here that we began to clear what we called Main Slope, bypassing the much steeper terrain directly above and below for the time being. Our method was to chop, saw or lop each tree or bush at or below ground level. For this reason a GI foxhole spade was an important part of the clutch of tools we carried uphill each time we began work.

I had never used an axe before so started out with a hatchet. Dave used a single-bitted axe with which he had had a bit of experience, mostly to split firewood. It wasn't long before we were both swinging heavier double-bitted axes, however. One blade was honed sharp for use when there was little or no danger of encountering dirt or rocks. The other blade was used for cutting close to the ground. We shared the spade, a bow saw, a wrecking bar, a sturdy pair of loppers and a whetstone for keeping the axes sharp. Cutting below or at least flush with ground level

---

[5] I am sorry to say that John was later found dead in his barn with a rope around his neck. The verdict was suicide, but the circumstances were suspicious. We were told that his feet could have reached the floor allowing him to stand up. It turned out, however, that he had recently bought a rope and said he was going to hang himself. That barn, almost a duplicate of Erma's which became the base lodge, later burned to the ground, also under suspicious circumstances.

added considerably to our workload because the circumference of most trees increases at or below ground level compared to a just few inches above the ground. This method of clearing was crucial to our success in the years before snowmaking because it enabled us to open for skiing on as little as six inches of snow on the grassy areas of Main and Lower Brewer. As we went on in the following years to develop more heavily wooded terrain, we sowed grass seed to provide cover for the soil.

Lugging a wrecking bar uphill along with the rest of the tools (and water and food) may seem odd. We used it for prying rocks out of the ground so we could throw them off to the side of the slope or trail we were working on. Rocks were even more of an impediment to good skiing (and skis!) than stumps and stubble so it was important to try to remove every one. The only problem was that this job was never finished because the frosts kept pushing more rocks to the surface. Not wanting to carry wrecking bars all the time, we went around for years with large screwdrivers sticking out of our back pockets even when engaged in other work at the time.

We also carried a gallon paint can half-filled with a solution of brush killer - sodium arsenite - and a paintbrush to apply it selectively to freshly cut brush and tree stumps. We were careful to avoid letting it touch our skin. I can remember one occasion when Dave insisted on pouring the fresh lemonade we were both looking forward to for lunch over my hand after I had made a grab for the paintbrush disappearing in the solution

In subsequent years, we resorted to using spray tanks worn over one shoulder, but were always very selective in spraying only the thick stands of woody growth we needed to rid of.

The wasteful timbering practices of the last century were unconcerned with topsoil retention. By the time we came along, the hillsides had only a very thin layer of it over the clay subsoil and shale bedrock. What little soil there was, was heavily laced with rocks, mostly chunks of shale, that had been stripped from the bedrock by the glacier. Later on, when we disturbed the earth with bulldozers, we hand-picked out the visible rocks, raked and seeded the unpromising soil and covered it with generous amounts of hay or straw to hold the seeds in pace and make the inevitable scraped spots in pre-snowmaking days less unfriendly to skis.

Most of this work was accomplished on weekends by staying with Aunt Nell (Eleanor Davison Robinson) on Canandaigua Lake, an hour's drive from Swain. By leaving at five a.m., we could be on the hill, grubbing away, by six. It was so fortunate that Aunt Nell and I took to each other because she had been like a third parent to Dave who had accompanied her to the lake for the summer even in his pre-school days. Everybody took to Aunt Nell who was full of good humor and kindness. It was part of her good nature to accept me if only for Dave's sake.

After working all day, we would return, tired and covered with dirt and sweat, and immerse ourselves in the lake. In those days, before the surge in the motor-boating population, the water was so clean we drank it directly from the lake or from one of the two pails we kept filled next to the kitchen sink. There was no running water, only a well, sulfurous enough to start a spa, located just outside the screened-in dining porch off the kitchen. Everybody preferred the lake water.

My recollection is that Dave and I did all the first year's clearing with our own four hands that first summer. It became a routine and we just buckled down and got on with it. Word of our project got around Kodak, however, and by early autumn, there was a day when a party of volunteers arrived to haul the brush and trees we had cut the previous day off into the woods. Whenever practical, brush was arranged along the west side of a slope or trail to break the west wind and serve as snow fencing to deposit snow on the trails. I'm not sure who all these most welcome people were at this point, but I know some later became members of the Swain Ski Patrol.

A little before this time, the Clark family became an important factor in getting the area up and running and an important part of our lives. Mary and Dick Clark were not the type to loaf around on weekends. They were accustomed to taking their children, David, Dianne, Bill and Gail camping. Dick was a scoutmaster with a lot of practical experience, and Mary, in addition to being a good cook, possessed many practical skills acquired in keeping their home up to snuff. Gail, the youngest, was only three or four years old when they became an indispensable part of the project as evidenced by the fact that the area's principal slope, originally dubbed Main Slope, became and remains Clark Slope.

The Clarks thought it would be fun to camp out in Swain and help out with whatever needed doing. Dick had acquired an array of practical engineering, mechanical and electrical skills that were to become invaluable. He and Mary both contributed a lot of good ideas and hard work

Besides being a dab hand with paint brush or rake, Mary ran the cafeteria at an Irondequoit school and was interested in the running the cafeteria at Swain. We started out collaborating on it, but she was so much more knowledgeable, and there were so many other things to be done, that I backed off and left it in her capable hands.

The children, I think David, the oldest, may have been 12 at the time, helped out with jobs like rope hauling, rock picking, hay spreading, etc. but had plenty of time to become acquainted and engage in activities with their contemporaries in Swain.

At night, we all slept on the floor of the drafty barn that was to become the base lodge. A former chicken coop, nothing like today's vast sheds crammed with thousands of immobilized chickens, became an outdoor privy divided into two sections, each with two holes. It would be the area's only toilet for the first year or two. I can't imagine skiers putting up with such conditions today, but skiers in those days were willing to put up with primitive conditions in order to spend more time skiing down than climbing up.

Water was lugged down the hill from a wonderful spring on Erma's land that served four nearby households. It was located about 100 feet above the valley floor A pipe rose maybe 3 ½ feet above the ground below the spring so there was plenty of room to fit a 5-gallon milk can underneath. Sticking out of the pipe was a rod that looked like an upside down "L." The "L" served as a handle to twist the rod around and open a valve down below the frost line allowing the water to siphon into the can from the mostly-buried spring house.

I had occasion to lift one of those old five gallon steel milk cans recently and was surprised how heavy it seemed even when empty. I was surprised to learn that it only weighed 25 pounds. Filled with water, it would have weighed 65 pounds, not too much for one person to carry back then, but we quickly learned that they were easy for two people to carry, by each taking a handle and leaning away from each other. It doesn't seem that this would actually lighten the load, but it seemed to, probably because we were leaning as much as lifting.

One of these cans, the outside now brown with rust, the tap at the bottom dulled but still silver, is at this writing topped with a pot of trailing flowers in front of our garage. Mary made do with two such cans during the peak of the lunch period. It must have been maddening as the flow became slower as the water level fell, but her camping experience had prepared her for coping with difficult conditions. In the second or third winter, Dick installed a stock watering tank above the double laundry tub sink in Mary's kitchen. It was filled by a hose, with water from the line which ran close by the "ski barn" en route to the house where Gunny (actually named Myrl, but I never heard him called that) Yencer lived with his wife Agnes and children, Marilyn, Terry and Linda.

This gravity-fed water system was a marvel of homespun engineering and hard work. Besides the five Yencers, it served John Brewer's house shared with Orsina ("Siney" Underwood) and Leon Spike and their 15 children (Ruth, Betty, William, Carl, Howard, Mary, Barbara, Geraldine, James, JoAnn, Thomas, Richard, Carolyn Jean, Daniel, Charles) and the homes of Erma Gleason Babcock and Anna and Ray Wirt. We were privileged to share the fruits of a lot of hard labor. Agnes and Gunny's daughter Marilyn Weidman recalls her father, John Brewer and Ray Wirt, three of the four home owners, digging ditches and installing pipe with their own six hands in 1935. In addition to building a stone and concrete reservoir around the spring, installing the system entailed digging supply lines to each house with pick and shovel, a total distance of over 600 feet, more than a tenth of a mile. Because the pipes were buried four feet deep, the lines never froze up even when the temperature dropped to 30 degrees below zero as it sometimes did.

Erma owned the land where the spring emerged. The Yencers lived next door and Ray and his wife Anna owned the fourth house, now occupied only by Marilyn Weidman, Lynn having recently passed on and their three children (Kevin, Linsie and Amy) now living elsewhere with their own families.

Getting back to the base lodge, the rest of the kitchen equipment consisted of a used grill, two simple countertop gas burners fueled by bottled gas and an old-fashioned two-compartment wash tub of the type used for rinsing clothes before automatic washing machines took over the job. These items, plus a used steam table procured by Mary, and our old GE monitor-top refrigerator remained through several renovations. They don't even hint at the area's modern gleaming stainless steel kitchen facilities that came later, but they helped keep people fed without running up more bills than we could pay.

As winter drew closer, the Clarks moved their compact camping trailer next to the base ledge for the winter so they had a regular place to sleep. I don't actually remember, but it seems that Dave and I must have slept on the picnic-type tables because the floor would have been wet from snow (and in the spring, mud) tracked in on people's boots After lugging gasoline, shoveling snow and serving as ski patrollers all day, we could have slept anywhere.

The base lodge that first winter consisted of two-thirds of the main floor of the barn. It was heated, not by a welcoming fireplace, but by a small bare metal kerosene stove, the business part of most such stoves in those days, but without the more presentable (and safer) surrounding metal jacket. As winter drew closer, we realized that we would not have time to enclose this area from the rest of the barn. That's when nearby Canaseraga contractor Gail Coombs came to the rescue. Explaining that we didn't have any money, we left the details to him.

Working much of the time in sub-zero cold, he sealed up the two sections of the barn that had solid flooring underfoot with ordinary sheetrock, practical and cheap but devoid of the rustic qualities we would have liked but couldn't afford. I remember once wailing when we arrived (Remember that we were both working at full time jobs and commuting from Rochester, three hours round trip, on weekends.) to find that he had even covered the old wooden barn beams which would have lent at least a touch of rusticity. Gail's objective was to hide the barn as much as possible making it seem more appropriate for human occupancy. He covered the outside with ordinary roll roofing to keep the wind out. He did a great job as cheaply as possible and trusted us to pay him when we could.

Gail's wife Winnie volunteered to paint two signs, one for either side of the junction of Main Street and what was then Route 408 and is now Route 70. They were about a square yard in size and consisted of rough scrap lumber covered with roofing material nailed to rough two-by-four posts. We painted the gray roofing green and Winnie did a creditable job of painting "Swain Ski Slopes" in white letters as large the area would accommodate. They served for the first few years. Winnie was later, after Gail had passed on and she herself was past normal retirement age, to become a trusted quad lift attendant in charge of chairs number one and two which ran side by side. Their sons Bob, Marty, Fran, Phil, and Ray have carried on their father's business.

December came around and we still didn't have the rope tow installed. A rope tow is nothing more than a long piece (in this case, over half a mile) of one-inch manila rope (We later used inch-and-a-quarter for easier grabbing and better wear.) with its ends spliced together to form a loop. Thanks to his wartime experience at sea, Dave was a skilled splicer. I can remember him performing this task bare-handed on several occasions, sometimes with spectators standing around to shield his bare hands from the cold air.

When it was time to haul the new rope uphill, the local children came to help without being asked. They stationed themselves at intervals appropriate to their size and strength, sat down and spent the afternoon hauling the rope up their section of the towpath.

Going uphill during regular operation, the rope either drags on the ground or is held up by skiers catching a ride. For the downhill journey, the standard practice at that time was to use old automobile wheels bolted to trees (or wooden telephone poles in places where no tree was handy) to guide the rope back to the motor where it was passed around a number of sheaves which served as sort of a gear box to transfer power from the motor's fast-spinning drive shaft to a much larger pulley, or drive-wheel that would propel the rope at a reasonable speed for skiers to grab and hang on to.

It is more efficient to have the motor pull from the top, but there are advantages to propelling the rope from the bottom such as avoiding the problem of getting the motor and the rest of the assembly up the hill in the first place. Another advantage would be being able to sell tickets from same building that housed the motor. Aside from transporting a lot of heavy equipment up hill, the big disadvantage of pulling from the top would be having to carry gasoline uphill to keep the motor supplied. All things considered, we opted to drive from the bottom that first year, which turned out to be a very good thing.

During the previous summer, we had commissioned a skiing friend with a contracting business in the Rochester area to produce the motor and necessary linkage to haul the rope and the skiers clinging to it to the top of the slope. The week before Christmas, the weather turned cold and snowy reminding us that we were late getting the area open, but no work had been done on motor and necessary linkage. Dave had taken a week's vacation from his job at Kodak. I was on vacation from Harley School where I was by then teaching girls' physical education.[6] The best we could do was hang out around the shop to make sure the contractor was getting on with the job we had commissioned several months earlier.

Probably to avoid our anxious questions, we were assigned the job of cleaning the solidified black grease from the ring bearings in a score or more of old automobile wheels procured from junkyards. This was done by dipping the bearings into an old chipped enamel dishpan full of gasoline and scrubbing them clean with a brush. In our greenness, we handled them as if they were pieces of jewelry, buffing each one until it had regained its original bright silver luster.

---

[6] Many of our meals consisted of leftovers from the school's family-style lunch program which were made available for faculty members to take home and use up. We did more than our share to implement this sensible waste-prevention.

The motor the contractor furnished came from an old "steam" shovel belonging to another contractor. The linkage consisted of items as diverse as an 8-inch coupling from a junk yard and a deluxe, machined-to-order steel drive wheel that was maybe 3 feet in diameter. It had three or four grooves to provide traction for the rope.

I remember accompanying a man named Chuck to several junkyards in search for a coupling with the right dimensions. He eventually found it under an ancient wooden-bodied Packard moving van, but not before he had slid under practically every other truck at that and several other junkyards.

Somehow, everything finally got put together and was picked up by Fred Blakley's crew, probably on their way back from delivering a load of lumber to the Morse Lumber Company in Rochester. I was to ride back on the truck for some reason, probably because Dave had had to return to his job and would drive down after work. There were four of us in the cab, which meant I had to sit on poor Junior Blakley's lap for about an hour and a half. Junior was Maude and Fred's teenage son who would have been on school vacation and had perhaps come along for the ride while learning his father's business. Carl Underwood was driving as usual. I think the fourth person was our neighbor Ernie Blakley, another member of the woods and sawmill crews.

Before we left, Chuck, who had found the critical coupling in the junkyard, took me aside and quietly warned me not to try to repair the motor if it ever stopped running. Caught up as I was in the excitement of finally being in possession of equipment to drive the tow, the ominous significance of this advice did not fully register with me at the time. I took it seriously enough to relay it to Dave as soon as I saw him again, however. We both must have relegated it to the back of our minds as something to worry about later as we got on with the business of installing the tow.

With just one tow to serve all comers that first year, we decided to build a platform for the motor a hundred feet or so above the bottom of the hill so that there would be a small slope with a separate rope running off the same motor to provide first timers the opportunity try out their ski legs before tackling a longer run. I don't recall its being used much. Nor do I recall how we got the steep hillside graded with a flat spot for the motor to rest on. The likeliest explanation seems to be that Fred Blakley did it for us, but it is possible that Lee and Bob Blades of A.L. Blades Construction in Hornell got involved that early.

Lee and Bob were both Dartmouth graduates and had been on Dartmouth's ski team. They were enthusiastic about having a place to ski with their families less than 20 miles from home. The area came along a lot faster after the first year because they generously loaned us one of their bulldozers with an operator during their slack periods for several years before we acquired a used bulldozer of our own.

Our arrangement with the Blades was to give their families free skiing in exchange for the work, a very advantageous deal for us as we were always short of money. We must have hired some of the bulldozing, however, as Marilyn Weidman recalls her father, Gunny Yencer, and Bill Pierce performing the bulldozing necessary to extend Clark (then Main) Slope to the valley bottom. She also recalls that Charlie Kreiley of Canaseraga handled the bulldozing to create lower Mile Sweep, a highway-like traverse across steep terrain, to bring skiers back to the lift from the trails on the east side of the area. These developments came much later, however.

I vividly remember laying the floor of the little building that was to house the motor for the first tow. We had worked all day at low temperatures in a foot or more of loose snow to complete an unfinished trail. Laying that floor was something we could do after dark by flashlight. We had discovered a cache of three-inch-thick oak planks in the basement of the barn that seemed just right for the job. We had also procured a box of heavy spikes long enough to go through the planks and into the floor joists already in place.

We pulled on our outer coveralls, which were probably still wet if not frozen, and got cracking. The first job was to carry the heavy planks, out of the basement, across the parking lot, which had been a cornfield just two months previously, and then a short distance uphill to the motor platform. This task had the benefit of getting us warmed up for the cold job ahead. If not below zero, the temperature must have been at least in single digits. It was COLD. I remember our breath forming little clouds in the still, moonlit air.

Our biggest hammer bounced off the spikes as if they had been made of rubber. Only the much heavier maul could drive a spike of that size into that well-seasoned white oak. Unable to wield the maul with one hand as Dave did, I developed a grotesque technique using both hands and bobbing up and down like one of those perpetually-drinking toy birds seen at fairs and souvenir shops. We took turns holding the flashlight and using the maul. A mis-hit resulted in a bent spike and usually starting over again with a new one, but we persevered and got the job done. A roof and walls were added later.

Our first day of operation came soon after. It was a disaster. After two hours, the motor quit never to run again. This was perhaps the lowest of the many low spots we had to endure. I am reminded of how really nice everybody was in those early days. No complaints. Some didn't even want to accept a refund of the dollar they had paid for their tickets. The fact we had perhaps as many as 20 customers on that first day was probably due to Rochester newspaper columnists John Brown and Floyd King.

Carl Underwood who was running the tow did not accept defeat so easily, however. He looked over the linkage between the motor and drive wheels. I don't remember everything exactly, but things began to happen, and happen fast. If Fred Blakley wasn't among the local spectators, he was summoned. He agreed with Carl, that the motor from the planer in the sawmill run by his brother Ben would fit the linkage between the motor and the drive wheel. Please bear in mind that I hardly knew most of these people in those early days, and everybody was bundled up to their noses in the similar heavy lumber jackets(aka mackinaws) worn for outdoor work in those days.

I don't remember who did what or the exact sequence of events but within another couple of hours, the defunct motor had been set aside, and a group of men were manhandling the planer's International motor up the slope on skids and installing it in place of the dead one. These men were used to working together, probably had been doing so all their adult lives, as well as having played together as kids.[7] They worked as one.

---

[7] As adults, they were a formidable softball team for the simple reason they could field and throw a hit ball with full confidence that a teammate would somehow always be there to receive it.

Even their voices were harmonious as they quietly exchanged information on who needed to do what as they strained to get the motor uphill. That motor must have weighed almost half a ton but they pushed and pulled and pried it up the snowy slope and into place as if the whole operation had been previously choreographed. My recollection is that the original motor died about 11 a.m. and the tow was running again by 2 p.m.

Everybody who had worked on the original motor must have known that the crank shaft was too worn to go on turning for long, but the Pittsford crew, except for Chuck, kept mum in deference to the boss. Neither Dave nor I had any mechanical experience beyond changing a tire or emptying a sediment bulb. Our new neighbors were too polite to suggest we had been taken, but they leaped to fill the breech when the need arose. I doubt we would have been able to operate at all that winter - and possibly never thereafter - if they hadn't. We had not only acquired land on which to build a ski area, but the backing of a community of self-reliant people who hardly knew us but knew how to make things work.

I don't remember anything else specific about that first season except that the ex-cornfield parking lot got awfully muddy in March. We hadn't wanted to deprive Fred Neetz of the use of that field for which he paid us the five dollars he had usually paid Erma. The mud was an inconvenience for our customers and the muddy floor didn't help the ambience of the base lodge. After the first year, we reluctantly had to cancel this arrangement to spare us all from the mud as the March sun crept higher and beamed down on the flat parking lot.

We were glad we didn't have to oust Anna France's pet sheep from the bottom of Mile Sweep a few years later after we were using more of the east side of the hill. Anna and husband Del, who put up and removed the fence posts according to the season, lived adjacent to that area with children Arthur, Dorothy and Dale. After the sheep's diligent mowing had assured the area of a thick crop of grass in a high traffic area, the small flock spent the winter on Anna's parents' farm up the valley.

Most of the local kids miraculously got skis from somewhere. They skied for free but were expected to help me with the side stepping to pack down the snow for an hour or so before the tow started, which they cheerfully did in conjunction with the little community's attitude of wanting to help. I gave them some basic instruction in making snowplow turns to get them started, but they took off from there and became good skiers just by doing what comes naturally to kids living next to a ski area.

Present outdoor slope manager, Harry Weaver who had somehow missed out on this arrangement, recently told me that Dave had given him the job of picking up coke bottles in the lodge and helping Duane ("Buster") Swain to set race courses in order to qualify for a free ticket.

For the first decade or so, the area was only open on weekends, holidays and school vacations because Dave and I had to work in the city to pay the bills. I must have stopped working at some point during that time because I remember being there during the week with Christie, our dog, and Bunker, our cat, just climbing up and down hill to pack in the snow. Christie (a collie named for Christiania turns, or Christies) and Bunker (a grey Maltese so named because he had been born in a coal bin) used to accompany me as I sidestepped up and down all morning and snow-shoed up and down all afternoon to compress the snow and help build up a base. On extra cold days, Bunker would alternately ride up and down on my shoulder or cuddle up with Christie who reveled in the snow in her heavy wool undercoat similar to that of a sheep.

We must have had a poor season sometime after that because I took a job with Stromberg Carlson in Rochester inspecting electrical parts to make sure they met specifications for one of their government contracts. I attributed a certain queasiness to job pressure but it turned out to be an announcement that the growth of our first child was underway and due to arrive in January. I resigned just before Christmas in order to be at the area for the holidays, but Challice didn't join us until Groundhog's Day, 1954.

The next phase of snow maintenance came with a used Ferguson tractor we were eventually able to buy for general work around the area. It was a dull gray color and I came to think of it as our "good grey Ferguson" in accordance with Time Magazine's then current commendatory appellation for older politicians warranting editorial approval. The tractor was fitted with Bombardier half tracks, a ladder-like assembly of metal cleats set in a thick rubber and fiber frame similar to the material in automobile tires, but a lot thicker.

The tracks linked the big back wheels to small idlers just behind the front wheels, giving it caterpillar-like traction as long as you kept going straight up or down slopes. Going sideways across a slope risked the wheels slipping out of the tracks. I can remember several occasions when whichever one of us was standing by had to throw his weight on the uphill side to prevent a rollover. The tractor couldn't climb steep slopes in snow, but did wonders just driving around on the flat as well as up and down gentler slopes. (In summer, it could mow steep slopes as long as it was headed straight downhill.)

The next step was to drag a weighted sledge or a rolling metal drum behind it. Dick Clark was especially clever at thinking up and constructing such devices. We also picked up a lot of good ideas by attending conferences and conferring with more established area operators in New England and the Adirondacks.

Specialized vehicles for maintaining snow were being developed but were beyond our means. The Bombardier, which looked and ran sort of like a military tank, was one of the earliest. We were later to acquire a used one but preferred the slower Tucker SnoCat with flat metal tracks which pressed the snow down more precisely. Either of these was beyond our still very limited means but we heard about and acquired a relatively light weight little Tucker that had been used for carrying meteorologists through deep snow to check weather observation stations somewhere. [8]

The first and fourth Tuckers had regular tracks in back, but the front consisted of a pair of skis controlled by the steering wheel. Except for a roof, the cab of the first one was open to the weather.

Many a snowy night I watched from a kitchen window as Dave drove down the almost vertical slope just opposite. It was like an aerial view because I seemed to be looking directly at the roof of the cab. We didn't have modern insulated clothing yet and the cab was open on the sides. Dave just piled on what he had. I remember he put his old merchant marine pea jacket over his knees leaving his feet free to work the controls.

---

[8] Daughter Challice recalls hearing more than once that these weather stations were at the North Pole, but I think somewhere in the Adirondacks is more likely. Then, Harry Weaver reminded me that we had later bought a fourth Tucker with a ski front that I had forgotten about. As this one was equipped with a cab for carrying passengers, the North Pole story seems more feasible.

Every two or three hours, he'd brush the snow off his clothes and come inside just long enough to down a hot chocolate. These were upbeat times because we were getting more snow and looking forward to good skiing the next day. I would be busy hand-stamping tickets or making chili for the cafeteria while keeping tabs on Dave to make sure he was OK.

Eventually, we were able to buy our first regular Tucker SnoCat and devices to draw behind it to chew up or pack down snow as conditions required. Not long after that, we acquired a second Tucker to meet the work load presented by the expanding trail system and to make sure that at least one, if not always two, was always capable of functioning.

The next step up was a Thiokol with a blade that could cut the tops off moguls that had become too difficult for even mogul enthusiasts to enjoy. Harry Weaver recalls that Dave was so impressed with it that he wanted to buy the demonstrator then and there, but we had to wait a few days for a new machine to be delivered.

Today's equipment works almost like a mill, taking in the upper layer of snow from the slopes and completely reprocessing it before redistributing and smoothing it down to provide a surface that helps everyone to ski better and enjoy themselves more.

Marilyn Weidman recalls severe snow conditions during which a SnoCat was used to bring milk down from the Whitney farm so it could be picked up while still fresh, and I remember a time when Dave drove Dave Swain back to his farm farther along Swain Hill after he had made his way down in a severe blizzard to procure a fuse to restore electricity (and heat) to his house. The road was lost in the swirling snow. They were able to find their way only by carefully following the wires from one electric pole to another. That was back before snowmobiles had come upon the scene, of course.

Getting back to the start of the early rope tow operation, Fred and Ben and the sawmill crew could not afford to do without their planer for the rest of the winter, but it just so happened that among other things, Fred was a dealer in International motors. He proposed ordering a new motor and selling it to us at his dealer's cost. That sounded wonderful except that we didn't have any money. Fred solved that problem by saying that he could wait until we had it.

As the area slowly expanded sideways and farther uphill, Fred later ordered another larger motor to drive another tow running alongside Main slope. The smaller motor was transferred to power two shorter tows for beginners' slopes on John Brewer's land. By then, we were more efficiently pulling the ropes uphill from the top instead of propelling them from the bottom as at first.

It's hard to imagine an astute businessman, which Fred certainly was, making an unsecured loan to a young couple he hardly knew who were engaged in a very high risk business. But Fred was a born entrepreneur, having developed a pea viner. De-viner would be a more description term as its purpose was to separate the pea pods from the vines.[9] A machine for manufacturing snow fence was among his other entrepreneurial projects. Fred liked to make things work and liked to see other people make things work. He was probably also motivated by a belief that a ski area would be good for the little hamlet of Swain.

---

[9] I can remember the big square pile of composting vines just outside of Canaseraga that would reach a height of six feet or more before a season's crop had been processed.

In the rope tow days, whoever was running the tows had to lift the rope onto hooks at the end of the day to give it a chance to dry out and unhang it while climbing uphill the next morning. Today, top of the hill lift attendants ride comfortably up and down sitting on the chairs or catch a ride with a snow groomer finishing a night's work.

The lifts' steel cables remain in place year round, unlike the old tow ropes which had to be laboriously hauled into the tow houses where they could be spared exposure to the weather during the off-season.

It would take Dave and me an entire weekend in the spring to lay out the ropes in long bights on the ground in preparation for hanging them under the roofs of the tow houses and another entire weekend in the autumn to restore them to their working positions. We could use the motor(s) to power the uphill haul, but you had to keep walking each bight uphill at a speed consistent with that of the motor. We took turns hauling rope and throwing the motor in and out of gear as needed. In some ways, hauling the rope downhill was easier because the motor wasn't involved. You just put it over your shoulder, leaned on it, and pulled until the friction and weight of the rope brought you to a stop. Then you climbed uphill for the next bight.

I can specifically remember putting the rope away in the spring of 1954 after Challice had joined the family in February. We carried her uphill in what was called a "car bed" (a far cry from today's safety provisions for transporting children). When it started to rain, we threw our windbreakers over her and put her under the raised floor of the tow house while we finished the job before the rope got too wet to put inside for the summer season.

Pulling the rope uphill from the top during the ski season was more advantageous mechanically, but had the serious disadvantage of making it harder to keep the motor supplied with gas. This chore fell to Dave, Dick Clark and me and I seem to remember Dave and Bill Clark and, occasionally even a customer, helping with this necessary job. It consisted of shouldering a knapsack with a five-gallon metal jerry can of gasoline inside. Inevitably, some gas got spilled on the canvas and our parkas smelled like gas pumps before the day was over.

This fuel delivery operation got really exciting when we all happened to be engaged in various critical tasks that caused us to delay the gas trip. Had the motor run out of gas at the top, which thankfully never happened, the pack would have had to have been walked up from the bottom while everybody waited for the tow to start up again. It is so different today with the lifts driven by electricity available at the flick of a switch and snowmobiles and other vehicles available to attend to other needs that arise.

The tasks that caused us to delay a refueling trip could have been something like assisting a skier who was hurt, conducting a ski lesson or shoveling fresh snow over a bare spot on the tow path. We had to be everywhere at once in those earliest days. Also, communication was difficult. At first, word from the tow operator that the gas tank was running low had to be delivered through the kindness of a passing skier and relayed to us.

It got easier after we installed phones and ran the necessary wires between the tow houses at the top and the ticket-selling booth at the bottom. The phones were powered by batteries. Turning a crank caused the phone at the other end of the line to ring signaling whoever was there to pick it up. Today, almost every ski patroller and key employee is equipped with a portable radio phone for intra-area communication. Ski patrollers can exchange information on their special channel about a skier possibly in need of help or something like a temporary "Trail Closed" sign now in need of removal.

Interestingly, the earliest cranked phones were the same type furnished to customers of Walt Kelly's Dalton Phone Company that served Swain. As a matter of fact, I think we bought the area's phones from Walt. Unlike our Rochester landlady who had assigned us 10 doorbell rings, Walt assigned a combination of long and short rings for each customer a la Morse code. In some places, the phone lines were strung on fence posts but they worked just as well as those strung overhead - except on the rare occasions when someone accidentally ran into them.

Dalton phone company customers could ring each other directly by observing the long-short codes. I think our ring was long-short-long followed by three shorts. The only problem was that it wasn't always easy to govern the length of the rings while cranking. Sometimes a long sounded like two shorts or two shorts like a long. An operator, usually Mildred Cromwell, but occasionally Walt himself, made the connection when someone needed to make a call outside the system. No dial tone then. An operator would take your call. Except in an emergency, everybody avoided making calls late at night and before six in the morning. When we were both still working at full-time jobs in the Rochester area, the operator kindly relayed snow reports to skiers when we were not there.

I think everybody in Swain was on the same line, but what a wonderful service Walt provided to people who might otherwise have been without phones for some years before Ma Bell got around to serving such a thinly populated area. On the other hand, she might have gotten to it sooner if Walt hadn't beaten her to it.

As we added new slopes and trails during the summers, it became advisable to relocate the main tow. Instead of mounting the return idler wheels on trees as we had done in the past, we built a set of what were essentially long-legged wooden saw horses. This was done in situ as it was easier to transport single planks than the unwieldy sawhorses, which were about 10 feet tall. This was before we had a tractor and was one of the times when our next door neighbor, Gunny Yencer used the tractor he had built from an old truck to help us out. He hauled the planks up hill and deposited them at intervals on the way down saving us a lot of heavy uphill lugging on foot.

The return idler wheels were mounted on the bar across the top of each sawhorse, affording the advantage of being able to move them from side to side to adjust the alignment. We nailed short pieces of one-inch scrap lumber up one of the uphill legs to serve as steps making it no longer necessary to carry a ladder to the site when the rope needed to be repositioned after it had bounced off a wheel. Fortunately, this didn't happen very often as skiers soon learned that it was not a good idea to ski out of the tracks.

At the end of a skiing day, the tension exerted on the rope by a block and tackle device at the bottom of the hill was released so the tow operator could hang the rope up to dry (or freeze) in the air as he walked down the hill. When it was time to start up again the next day, whoever was around, including skiers waiting to ride up, would put the tension back on the rope by hauling on a block and tackle. This was done with the participants alternately hauling and getting a new grip on the rope in the best seamanlike fashion. I can remember Bill Wadsworth, scion of a politically-influential, land-owning family of Geneseo, once remarking as he participated in the ritual, that his wiry build would make up for any lack of weight on his part.

In those early days, I seemed to be the one selling tickets and communicating with the operator at the top when necessary. It was a big relief when Phil Isaman (pronounced "eyes man") took over that job. We were told that the unusual combination of spelling and pronunciation was the result of a disagreement in the preceding century between two brothers named Eisaman. The disagreement was a heartfelt one, serious enough to cause one of them to disassociate himself from the other by changing the way he spelled his name. Both spellings persist in descendants living in the area.

After a decade or so, Phil and wife Norma bought a farm between Swain and Dalton and moved there with children Arlen, Phyllis, Bradley and Shirley. This meant Phil would no longer be available for selling tickets. The job was taken over by neighbors Barb and Ted Swain, who by then lived with their son Shawn immediately behind the base lodge in what had been Erma Gleason Babcock's house. By then, tickets were sold in the base lodge rather than at the foot of the lifts. This was a far cry from Ted's first job which had consisted of making sure everything continued to go well at the top of a lift before there was a building there. This must have been the year our first T-bar was installed. One really cold day, Ted built himself a fire from fallen wood and gained the reputation with skiers as being a professional woodsman when in reality he was the man in charge of the Erie Railroad depot in nearby Canaseraga.

The first day of the season after the first T-bar was installed was one of triumph cut short by sorrow. The T-bar, built and installed by engineer

Vic Hall and crew of Watertown, fulfilled our initial dream. It was installed right where I had visualized it on our first trip through Swain. I had to get the news of how wonderful the new lift was from others because I was too busy in the base lodge to steal time for even one ride. It was one those beautiful sunny winter days. The snow conditions were great. Customers and employees were full of joy and satisfaction, especially Ski Patrol Leader Dick Clark, who would no longer have to pull toboggans up hill behind him while hanging on to a tow rope.

The sorrow came at the end of that day's trail sweep. While exulting with friend and fellow ski patroller Ray Meyering, Dick suddenly fell over in the middle of a word. Ray was a New York State Trooper trained in emergency medical treatment. He did everything he could, but Dick had apparently died instantly of a massive heart attack. It was devastating for his family and everybody else. My heart went out to Mary who sat stunned and silent in Agnes Yencer's kitchen while the necessary medical and legal formalities were taken care of. Officials were not readily available for some reason. Dick's body lay stretched out on the floor while local people tried to get hold of them. Marilyn Weidman recalls getting stuck while she and Bernie Newmark tried to reach Dr. Tisdale's house on a steep hillside.

It was such a bolt from the blue that the children didn't seem to have completed the plunge all the way from cloud nine into tragedy as they rallied round their mother. All I could do was fix them some hot food before they left for home. At the patrol's suggestion, what had been Main Slope became Clark Slope from that day on.

In the earliest years when we did all the clearing with hand tools, the hill below Main / Clark Slope was too steep for us to handle. Come to think of it, we had yet to acquire access to that land. We might possibly have devised a way to remove the trees with our own hands, but it was unlikely that we could have smoothed with mere pick and shovel the almost vertical pitch of bedrock and heavy clay soil interlaced with tree roots.

For that reason, traffic was at first diverted to the west down Run Off, an old farm road, to where the valley carved by Ewart Creek had allowed the glacier to spread out resulting in a gentler grade just above the valley floor. The lower extension of Main Slope (now Clark Slope) invited the development of more trails on the east side of the hill where we had acquired a tract of land from Ben Blakley. One of the trails was named after him, but somehow none was ever named after his brother Fred,[10] who was such a big factor in getting the area going.

It was probably the year that the T-bar was installed that Clark Slope was extended all the way to the bottom of the hill. The job was accomplished by Gunny Yencer and Bill Pierce using two bulldozers. Gunny's daughter Marilyn recalls that the area had acquired its own used bulldozer by then and that Bill operated the town dozer. That was probably the job for which I remember paying the Town of Grove $200.

More extensive bulldozing performed by Charlie Kreiley of Canaseraga across the steep lower pitch on the east side of the hill created a wide, gently sloping highway that enabled novices to negotiate the steep pitch of the lower valley wall. 80-Acre Slope, Ben Blakley, Promenade and Dozey Doe all spilled onto this highway, but most importantly, it

---

[10] Daughter Janet says: "I distinctly recall that Fred didn't want a trail named after him. He said, 'Name it for my brother.' Not that I remember Fred saying it, but I remember Dad saying so."

permitted the development of Mile Sweep, a gentle, mile-long elbow that wound around the east side of the area giving novices a long, gentle run.

All areas where the earth was disturbed were given the same treatment. First, we raked down the soil to eliminate rocks and any ridges left by the bulldozer. Then, we carefully seeded with annual rye and creeping red fescue and applied a generous covering of straw. The rye provided quick cover to hold the soil in place while the fussier fescue was getting established. Red fescue was many times more expensive than other grass seeds, but once started, it seemed to thrive in heavy clay soil and formed a thick cover that obligingly bent over forming a thick mat that did not need to be mowed.

One summer a mother fox fashioned a home for her brood on this soft cushion of grass next to the woods at the bottom of the headwall on Clark Slope. Their domicile was screened by a healthy stand of golden rod. There were separate areas for playing, sleeping, and defecating. We left the stand of golden rod unmowed until just before winter when I walked up and snipped it out with hand clippers.

Mowing was first accomplished with a Cunningham walk-behind, three-foot sickle-bar mower, which ran on gasoline. It served us well for several years before we had the luxury of a tractor that mowed wider swaths while the operator sat in relative comfort on the metal seat. Except for the steepest pitches, the little Cunningham could climb up hill with a minimal amount of pushing, but was entirely free-wheeling on the descent, restrained only by the friction generated by the cutting bar. Going downhill with the cutting bar raised when not cutting meant the operator was either digging in heels to hold back or running wildly downhill to keep up with the machine - quite good sport for a skier.

Working close to the ground on foot resulted in carefully-groomed slopes which contributed greatly to successful operation in those early years before snowmaking became a factor. In later years, I couldn't help but noticing from the luxury of riding up on a chairlift that men operating sophisticated grooming equipment would run over rather than climb down to toss a small fallen branch off the slope. Such objects probably appeared less significant to a man riding high on a grooming machine than to someone on skis or foot. Also, it was probably a matter safety, as well as efficiency as parking on some of the steeper slopes could be hazardous to both man and machine. Still, it shows that there is something to be said in favor of doing things the old fashioned way as members of the ski patrol still do.

Here endeth my stream of consciousness account of the earliest days. The following chapters will give more details on how various aspects of the area progressed. The final chapter will discuss Swain's past and how the ski area affected this little backwater community.

Trail and Slope Development

I covered our method of clearing trails with hand tools in some detail in the previous chapter and won't repeat it here. This chapter will be more a simple historical account of the sequence of the trail network development

The days when Dave and I carved out slopes and trails with hand tools gradually came to an end, but I can't say exactly when this came about. I remember we continued to lay out where the trails would go for some years after we were able to pay others to help with the actual cutting. This brings to mind an occasion, probably in the month of May sometime in the early 1950's, when we were just setting forth to lay out a trail to be cut for the next season.

As was our custom on such occasions, we were each wearing a belt festooned with bunches of yard-long strips of knitted fabric in pastel colors[11] that we used to mark the edges of the trail-to-be when who

---

[11] The strips were furnished free of charge by Marion Rohr, a Hornell factory run by one of our customers, Henry Schlossberg. The factory specialized in producing women's underpants. The narrow strips were what was left over after cutting through 150 layers of fabric at a time. Henry informs me that each cutting provided pieces for 48,000 pairs that would wind up all over the world.

should drive into the parking lot but Dr. Allan Harder of Hornell, who was always on call for the ski patrol. He was showing another doctor, a prospective addition to the roster of Hornell medical practitioners, some of the amenities of the Hornell area and Swain was one of them. We all had a good laugh about the native customs and costumes.

As I confessed in the introduction, my concept of time past is not always well defined. I can't always be sure whether something happened 20 years ago or 30 years ago. Also, as the business grew, my efforts became concentrated on the ski shop, rental department and food service. It's harder to recall developments with which I had less hands-on experience. Having said that, I'll just set down events as best I can.

To start with, we sensibly took advantage of the least heavily wooded areas for the first slopes and trails. Our resolve to remove every rock and cut every tree and other woody growth at or below ground level made for slow progress. It paid off in the long run, however, because it enabled us to open on less snow during the critical early years before snow making became a factor.

Most of our work that first spring and summer consisted of removing maybe 30-years' growth from what is now the middle section of Clark Slope. We started just below the heavily forested upper headwall and worked down to a graded farm road which wound up at what was to be the base of the first rope tow. Bear in mind that we were both living and working full time in the Rochester area so that all this work had to be accomplished on weekends and holidays.

When we reached the bottom of the less heavily wooded area that Mark Heath had once cleared for farming, we funneled what was to be Main (later Clark) Slope into three much narrower trails through a more densely wooded area to connect with the farm road, thus avoiding for the time being the cliff-like terrain just above the valley floor that we were not equipped to handle. The trails, which were later absorbed by Main/Clark Slope were named Shawmut, Pine and Run Off. The name Pine was later transferred to another trail.

The lower third of John Brewer's land was mostly grass-covered. Too steep for plowing, it had been used for pasture and had very little woody growth. It gave us a second, shorter slope in exchange for chopping a passage through the heavy hedgerow at the bottom. I remember Bill Whitney mowing it for us that first year with a team of two horses, one white, the other black.

This was a very minimal beginning, but gave people the most tow-serviced skiing available in western New York at that time. Also, unlike the two smaller areas operated by the Burby Hollow and Ellicottville ski clubs, Swain was open to the public. It was within an hour or two's drive of both the Rochester and Buffalo metropolitan areas, but it didn't take long for other areas to spring up with the advantage of being closer to these major markets. Our Buffalo, Canadian and Ohio customers naturally opted to ski closer to home when given the opportunity to do so, but the overall growth in the number of skiers gradually compensated us for the decline in customers from these areas.

In the beginning, Brewer Slope (named for its former owner John Brewer) used only about a third of its total possible elevation. It was probably in the second or third year that we were able to install two rope tows, driven by the same motor, on the western side of the slope. For the benefit of beginners, one of these ended before the pitch steepened. The other ended atop a natural plateau on which the tow house was built.

I recall using the rear end from a dual-tired truck to haul the two ropes uphill. The ropes rested in the grooves between the tires which provided excellent traction without the expense of machining a drive wheel. This arrangement was probably an idea we picked up from visiting other areas, but it could have been the brainchild of Fred Blakley or possibly the idea Dave mentioned acquiring from Ed Taylor.

After the ropes were replaced with T-bars, a small T-bar with non-retractable sticks ran up the middle of the Brewer to the plateau. This had the effect of dividing the slope so that novices had the west side to themselves leaving the east side more open for skiers descending from the steeper area above. By that time we had expanded Brewer to cover at least two-thirds of the hill. Brewer was cleared in three stages and I am not clear on exactly when the two expansions took place.

The narrow valley carved by Ewart Creek widened considerably before it joined the main Canaseraga Creek valley, but it was still narrow at the west side of Brewer. Its sides rose abruptly to form a shoulder that protected the north-facing lower slope from the west wind. On land acquired from Herthel and Alton Spencer, we cut a gently-sloping trail called Roundtop. In addition to giving skiers a somewhat longer run, it provided the option of avoiding the steeper pitch just below the plateau. It has always been popular with beginners and skiers who prefer a leisurely speed.

After our time, when T-bars totally gave way to chairs, two quads were installed side by side up the middle of the slope. The quads followed the original T-bar plan of having one end atop the plateau while the other continues to the top. Brewer, Wheels and Glenn's took off on the east side and Robinson and Last Will dropped, temporarily out of sight, on the west side. A gentle highway runs downhill toward the east from the top of the longer lift affording easy access to all the other slopes and trails. Access to Robinson's requires only a few pole thrusts and Last Will just a few skating strides.

Last Will, short for Last Will and Testament, was the prize-winning name for this steep slope. The unknown person who submitted it to the trail-naming contest was never rewarded because all the letters submitting names somehow managed to disappear. We kept expecting the winner to come forward to claim the season pass that was to be awarded to the winner, but he or she never did, and neither of us could remember the name which was not a familiar one. We never learned whether the winner had moved away or was making a charitable contribution to the financially struggling area by not claiming the promised prize.

Individual skiers have different slope or trail preferences, but Clark, probably because of its somewhat gentler mid-section and less precipitous headwall, seems to be the general favorite.

Rattler, just east of Clark, is more challenging, 80-Acre, on the other side of Rattler, a bit less so. Mile Sweep affords a more leisurely run ending in a wide boulevard. 80-Acre, Ben Blakley, Dozey Doe and Promenade spill into the same boulevard for an easy descent to the Clark quad or the double chair.

Pine Trail, just west of Clark, affords the best access to all four lifts. An almost vertical drop we named The Chute used to deposit skiers at the base of the double chair and the Clark lift, but it was later eliminated for some reason I don't recall. Pine has been widened in recent years to encompass a sculpted terrain park for the benefit of snowboarders who perform some remarkable aerial feats there. Continuing farther west along the steep north side, Glenn's and Wheels' (named for two young instructors killed in a car crash on their way to an evening out) lie between Pine and Brewer followed by Robinson and Last Will. A gentler, north-facing trail, ZigZag was closed after we had retired because it was difficult to groom. Glenn's, Wheels' and Robinson were cut after we had retired and had time to enjoy them.

Swain with a vertical drop of slightly over 600 feet is small compared to large destination areas but offers a lot of variety making it necessary to arrange a meeting time and place for skiers of the same party who choose not to stick together.

I can remember laying out and clearing the upper trails on the east side, including the original narrow version of Mile Sweep, and I can remember laying out ZigZag[12] on the west side, which Harry Weaver recalls clearing with axes.

I remember clearing one of the steep upper slopes, probably 80-Acre, with the several members of the sawmill crew, all of us using hand axes. It was raining, but the work had to go on because it was a weekend and

---

[12] Despite being a popular trail, ZigZag was abandoned after our time, probably because it was too narrow for the ever-larger grooming equipment. Also, the Z-shaped bends on the steep terrain required the groomers to traverse back and forth sideways, a trickier operation than heading straight up and down. Swain has always placed a high priority on having well-groomed trails and slopes so it made sense to abandon a trail that had become hard to groom.

the men would not have been free to work on the weekdays. That was the occasion on which I got tired of peeling soggy tissues off my wet fingers and scraping used ones back into a different pocket, and adopted the more practical habit of blowing my nose onto the ground like the rest of the crew. It somehow seemed less repugnant after I started doing it myself.

Most of the hand-cleared areas were later expanded using machine-age equipment. On new trails, the trees were pushed over and uprooted and the area smoothed ready for raking and seeding in days instead of weeks and months. We had taken in enough money to catch up with the 20th century - or maybe its demands had caught up with us.

Tows and Lifts

Downhill skiing can be an exhilarating experience provided free to all by the force of gravity. A steep slope can give the skier an airy sensation, a little like flying, even though his skis remain for the most part in contact with the ground. Even slower speeds on gentler slopes provide a pleasurable gliding sensation. In order for individuals to partake of these pleasant sensations, it used to be necessary to laboriously lug skis uphill or sidestep or herring bone back uphill while still attached to them. The time and effort invested in climbing for a relatively brief downhill experience was enough to discourage all but the most enthusiastic participants.

Not surprisingly, villages with sightseeing lifts in the Alps became meccas for recreational skiers. As the sport gained in popularity, it led to lifts being built expressly for the purpose of hauling skiers uphill. The most rudimentary of these was the rope tow. Rope tows being the cheapest to build and install, that's what we started with at Swain.

The first rope tow in the United States was built by local residents of Woodstock, Vermont in 1934. It was powered by an old Model T Ford Engine and led to the development of an area called Suicide Six, which with modern adaptations, is still going strong. If memory serves me correctly, its operator, Bunny Bertram devised a "shovel-handle" tow by attaching handles to the rope for skiers to grab onto. I have been unable to find out how the handles didn't jam up going around the drive wheel and return sheaves but surmise it may have had something to do with steep pitch of the hill that prevented the rope from twisting because it didn't touch the ground, but that is just conjecture on my part.

While a big improvement over mere arms and legs, rope tows were by no means effortless. Many a skier's day ended when his hands and arms were no longer up to the task. Rope tows did have one big advantage, however: speed. While they could be run at slow speeds for novices, they could be speeded up considerably so that experienced skiers could spend less time riding up and more time skiing down - for as long as their arms held out.

Chairlifts are almost essential for longer runs on higher mountains but are less practical for shorter runs because the luxury of a more comfortable ride on a chair has the disadvantage of taking more time. When the distance of the ride up approximates the length of the run down, the skier spends much more time sitting comfortably in the sun or shivering in the winter wind than he does skiing down. This disadvantage has been to a large extent overcome in recent years by designing lifts that slow down in the loading and unloading areas so that they can be run at higher speeds for the rest of trip. Some offer a wind shield that can be pulled down after getting underway.

Even with today's high lift-ticket prices necessary to pay for more sophisticated lifts, few skiers would opt to return to ropes. Depending on the day's conditions, the rope can become wet or icy, making it hard to get a grip as it slides through your gloves. When the temperature is above freezing on a delightful sunny day in March or April, squeezing the rope to get a grip tends to wring out the water which them creeps up your sleeve. Sometimes it even wound up running down the inside of the legs of the make-shift ski clothing of the early days in the 1940's.

One of the first items we sold along with tow tickets was a rope-tow gripper invented and marketed by Clare Bousquet who started an area with rope tows in my home town of Pittsfield, Massachusetts.[13] The gripper consisted of a simple clamp attached, at first by a few inches of ordinary cotton clothesline, to a sturdy white web belt. The metal clamp was like a big door hinge except that it was shaped both to afford a comfortable grip and to fit around the tow rope without unduly pinching and cutting into it. Once the skier was moving at the same speed as the rope, the clamp was positioned at right angles to the rope making it easier to hang on to than the fast- running rope which could slide through your gloves and leave you behind if you relaxed your grip. The belt had a pocket, and, later, a wide band of elastic webbing to hold the metal clamp when it was not in use. The gripper sold for $3.00 when tow tickets cost $1.50.

---

[13] According to their internet account, Bousquet's got its start when some members of the Mt. Greylock Ski Club asked for permission to practice skiing on the slopes rising above the family farm. Climbing up and skiing down was getting to be popular. This happened at a time when Clare was in danger of losing the farm as a result of the depression. There was no charge for skiing, but Clare and family made a little money from selling food. People came from as far away as New York City. After a rope tow was installed (for which there was a charge, of course) the New York Central ran special "snow trains" from New York City on weekends. I can remember once going with my parents to watch the crazy New Yorkers getting off the train. The bridge over the railroad siding was lined with spectators watching women in fur coats and high-heeled shoes milling around in the snow collecting their equipment, a source of interest as well as amusement for local people. The same thing happened when we first opened at Swain. A much shorter line of locals lined up behind a strip of snow fence at the base of the hill to be entertained by seeing people ski for the first time.

Good manila rope was expensive ($1.00 a foot comes to mind but I can't vouch for that figure which just popped into my head; half that amount seems more likely.) Whatever the exact cost was, rope was a major expense when you needed a mile of it and it had to be replaced every two or three years depending on how much it was used. Ideally, on a short, steep slope, a tow can be constructed to match the slant from top to bottom so that the rope does not drag on the ground, but this is not practical for tows serving longer slopes, especially those with varying pitches.

Another disadvantage of rope tows is that the tow path tends to wear out in places, especially when the temperature is above freezing as it often is in March when some of the otherwise best conditions occur. This means that it is desirable and sometimes really necessary to have someone with a shovel throwing snow on spots in need of it. I can remember times when a tow was able to run all day only because of Dick Blowers' heroic shoveling. I can also remember times in the afternoon when I went out hoping to get in an hour's skiing only to find that no one was shoveling for some reason such as a more pressing need elsewhere. At those times I would forego having a few runs and spend all the time I could afford away from the base lodge shoveling snow onto the towpath to improve conditions for our customers.

From the operator's point of view, in addition to being much less costly, ropes have the advantage of being relatively easy to install and move around to suit new trail developments. The hardest part is moving the motor and building, which have to be mounted on log skids so they can be pulled to the new location. This was not a job to be undertaken lightly, but the fact it could be done was helpful with our continually developing trail layout. Lifts with overhead cables, on the other hand, require substantial steel towers set in a substantial concrete base whereas ropes are held up by skiers on the uphill journey and only need something like old automobile wheels mounted on trees or poles to complete the circuit back to the motor.

At one point after Clark Slope had been extended to the top of the hill, we simply added a temporary extension to the existing tow using Fred Blakley's tractor as a source of power. It had a limit of three skiers at a time because of the steep pitch but ran so fast that I don't ever recall there being a waiting line. One winter day when the area was not open, Dave, Dick Blowers, Carl Underwood and I were working in and around the tow house. We were all home having lunch when Dick looked up and noticed the tow house was on fire.

He phoned Carl and us to meet him at the bottom of Clark. We all rode up clinging to the little Snocat, and each other in some cases, to find that the tow house was beyond saving. It seems we must have lost the motor too but I can't really recall whether or not that was the case. What I do recall is that flames had yet to reach Fred's tractor sitting next to the tow house and how Dick disconnected it, got on, started it up and drove it to safety with the back of his coveralls on fire. Thankfully the flames were doused before they could burn him.

The rope tows enabled us to get the area going, but we had had a T-bar in mind from the very beginning. After we had accumulated almost enough money, largely through the sale of stock, to fulfill our original dream, we were attracted by the low price offered by a western firm. The two partners who designed the lift, traveled east to sell us on its merits and stayed overnight with us when we were still living in Honeoye Falls. I remember that occasion because they were Mormons who drank neither coffee, tea nor beer and I was unable to respond to their request for soda.

Before making such a major investment, which could make or break the area, Dave felt he had to see more than photos and invested in a plane ticket to see the lift in operation. He was not impressed. Like us, the two partners were getting by on a shoestring budget. Their lift resembled something we might have cobbled together ourselves.

As a result, we paid more money for a more substantial T-bar manufactured and installed by Hall Engineering of Watertown, New York. It was a wise decision. Vic Hall oversaw the installation by his crew and the lift ran without a hitch until it was later dismantled (and resold) to make way for the first quad chair.

T- bars and the less common J-bars (which carry a single skier) work by steadily boosting skiers leaning against them to the top. They have one advantage over chairlifts: allowing skiers who prefer not to go to the top to get off along the way. In the days before significant improvements in ski equipment and snow grooming machines, this enabled skiers to avoid the steeper headwall on Clark if they wished to do so.

The biggest drawback to T-bars, from both the operator's and the skier's perspective, is that, depending on snow conditions, the lift path requires maintenance. This is probably the main reason why more expensive chair lifts have been replacing T-bars even on shorter slopes where a comfortable ride up is of less importance.

Before acquiring enough money for the first chairlift, we had installed four T-bars to cover the expanding trail system and reduce the time skiers had to wait in line on busy weekends. The first T-bar ran up the west side of Clark for almost 30 years before it was replaced after Dave and I had retired by the third of the three quad chairlifts installed by Robin Smith. The second T-bar, erected by Gunny Yencer using parts furnished by Hall Engineering, ran up the middle of lower Brewer. The third ran up the east side of Brewer after that slope had been extended all the way to the top.

The fourth T-bar, which was reached from the upper slopes, served upper 80-Acre, Rattler, Upper Mile Sweep and the three trails between them. It began at the junction where these trails spilled onto the boulevard of Lower Mile Sweep. It was installed primarily to help reduce waiting lines at the other three lifts but most skiers preferred to wait in line for a longer run even though the upper trails often offered the best snow conditions. It only ran on busy days but there was rarely a waiting line of more than three or four skiers. It was very popular with skiers who preferred to keep skiing just the upper two-thirds of the area rather than waiting in line for a longer ride up from the bottom.

The first chairlift, a double, was engineered and installed by Boris Borvig Ski Lifts. Its installation in 1970 was accomplished with the help of his stepson Gary Shulz, and contractors Bob Blenis and crew from New Jersey, Walt Sturdevant of Wellsville and Blackie Deebs of Hornell. The fact that it is still running on its original cable is solid testimony to Boris's design, the accurate work of the contractors, and, not least, the careful maintenance mostly conducted by Lyle and Harry Weaver – under several managers until Harry officially assumed the top job.

This chair runs at a slight diagonal from the lowest elevation at the bottom of Clark Slope to what was at that time the highest on top of Brewer, thus providing access to all preexisting slopes and trails. Robinson and Last Will, installed later, are just a little further along and can be reached with minimal effort.

Because it doesn't have to allow enough time for four skiers to line up for loading, "the double," can be run faster than the more modern quads making it a favorite with energetic skiers because it enables them to get in more downhill runs. Also, the swinging start and sense of being airborne provided by a lighter chair makes it more fun to ride than the more substantial, higher capacity quads.

The other three lifts are all quads (with a capacity of four instead of two skiers to a chair) and have to run at a somewhat slower speed in order to allow enough time for four skiers to get into position to be picked up. One of the quads replaces the original T-bar on the west side of Clark Slope. The other two, installed between Brewer and Robinson, follow the plan of the earlier T-bars. One runs all the way to the top. The other, propelled by a different motor, runs at a slower speed and deposits skiers on the natural plateau above Lower Brewer.

The lifts tie all the slopes and trails together enabling skiers to get from one to another easily and take advantage of the varied terrain allowing skiers to choose a different run every trip if they choose to do so.

Snowmaking

The knowledge that expanding sprays of water droplets cool and turn into snow or ice in below freezing air was free for anyone to take advantage of. Swain was not the first ski area to do so, but was one of the earliest to make use of this phenomenon to manufacture snow. Nowadays, even areas at high altitudes out west that measure snowfall in feet rather than inches, have installed snowmaking systems to compensate for less snow on lower slopes, get an earlier start on the ski season, and improve conditions after a thaw.

A Floyd King "Through the Skioscope" column in the Rochester Democrat and Chronicle's edition of January 22, 1956 describes a successful weekend made possible by man-made snow. Entitled "Swain Artificial Snow Proves Success," it read:

"Almost every ski area in Northeastern United States and Canada was washed out of business last weekend by the prolonged January thaw. Those that operated did so mostly on ice and listed conditions as poor.

"One of the exceptions was Swain Ski Slopes where the largest crowd in its history enjoyed excellent skiing on corn snow, framed by a Grandma Moses

winter wonderland of blue sky and ice-sheathed trees that sparkled in the sunshine like jewels.

"All this was the result of nature's prodigality and man's ingenuity. A freezing fog had mantled the entire Nunda area in ice, even the weeds in the fields glistening like fairy wands. The snow was man made - Swain's introduction to artificial snow. With temperatures just below freezing, the picture postcard hills and groomed trails made for a tremendously successful weekend. To Dave and Bina Robinson who had literally hewed Swain Ski Slopes out of the rugged, wooded hills, goes credit for introducing artificial snow to this area. They had been working on the project for two years and last week snow fell on Swain under a barren sky.

"The Robinsons drilled a deep well that apparently tapped an inexhaustible source of water. They installed a compressor that compresses air to high pressure. The water and compressed air are carried up the hill in twin aluminum pipes and discharged side by side in special nozzles. The result is a stream of snow crystals that shoots out into the air about 30 feet.

"Last week the Robinsons laid down a heavy base at the foot of the slopes where skiing pressure is heaviest and then sprayed a 60-foot swath up Lower Brewer Slope. This is the most used area as it combines intermediate and novice grades. The snow held up much better than nature's own under two days of heavy traffic.

"Dave estimated he can cover the entire skiing area with a six-inch snowfall in a week's time when he gets the equipment into full operation. He started replenishing the slopes in midweek and Swain is all set for a repeat performance this weekend unless temperatures shoot above freezing.

"Skiers found the artificial product excellent in every respect. It is granular in texture and very fast similar to spring skiing. They found turning almost as easy as on a packed surface. Most important was its wearing qualities. Even after two days of scraping, there were no large areas of bare ground showing through."

The actual production was handled by Gunny Yencer who is shown in an indistinct photo making adjustments to the system while daughter Marilyn stands by holding her skis in an artificial pose as directed by the photographer. Also, I should point out that, depending on the temperature and the ratio of air to water, snow can be made in almost any form from the granular ("corn") snow Floyd described to dry powder.

In the beginning, there were no engineering firms that we knew of offering their services to install snowmaking systems. We bought our first aluminum irrigation pipe from Larchmont Engineering, a Massachusetts firm specializing in farm irrigation systems that had hit upon another application for their sections of link-together aluminum tubing and eventually developed the know-how to engineer snow-making systems. Up to that point, you just had to figure a way to bring compressed air and water together where you wanted the snow to fall. The compressed air expanded forcibly as it left the nozzle at the end of the pipe causing the water issuing from an adjacent pipe to vaporize into fine particles. If the surrounding air was cold enough (below freezing and preferably below 26 degrees F.), the vaporized water became snow before it hit the ground. As you might imagine, a lot of experimenting was done with nozzles and determining the most efficient mix of water and air, a process it seems safe to assume is probably still going on at ski areas everywhere.

Our first need was an air compressor. Friendly fellow skier Bernie Newmark, who broadcast reports of ski conditions for Rochester area skiers, solved that one by locating four old compressors no longer used and kept in storage by the city of Rochester. It seems impossible today, but I think the city was glad to unload them for $400 each. This made us the owners of four compressors with electric motors to drive three of them even though our electric service lacked the force to do so at that time. The next step was to fetch them from the grassy bank beside the Erie Railroad tracks where they had been pushed off a train. All we had were crow bars, jacks, and. of course, our own four hands plus our sturdy little Ferguson tractor, much too small and underpowered for the job, but as game as we were. Today, almost every small farm has a much more powerful tractor whether they actually need it or not.

Each compressor and motor to drive it, was mounted on a sturdy metal frame. My recollection is that each assembly weighed two tons although that figure seems too high in retrospect. The first step was to mount each assembly on wooden skids to avoid tearing up the town road on the way to the Brewer barn where the compressors would be stored temporarily. The total distance we had to drag them was only about four tenths of a mile but the hard going made it seem more like four miles.

I don't remember why the compressors weren't delivered by truck from Rochester and unloaded next to the barn. It may have been because they were too heavy. Maybe it was because we didn't have suitable equipment to unload them although it seems in retrospect it would have been easier to build a ramp for that purpose than drag them from the railroad bank. Whatever the reason was, we had to deal with four pieces of heavy equipment sitting on a bank alongside the railroad tracks. Fortunately, the bank was on our side of the tracks eliminating the need to get the compressors across the tracks where getting stuck could have been disastrous for all concerned not least the crew of the next train to come along.

Once we had pried a unit up and fastened it to the logs that served as skids, the next step was to chain the assembly to the tractor's drawbar. Dave's wartime experience with loading heavy equipment for shipment overseas stood us in good stead here. Because the tractor was much lighter than its load, it took a bit of experimenting to determine the best distance between drawbar and load. When whoever was driving started to pull, the immediate reaction of the tractor was to rear up like a horse on its hind legs, in this case, its rear wheels. This was the case every time we had to start up after re-hitching numerous times to accommodate varying terrain as we avoided the road as much as possible. We took turns driving the tractor and easing the starts by prying up the front of the load with the crowbar, with Dave doing most of the rigging.

I remember the smell of the wooden skids getting hot, smoking and developing red coals on their surface where there was no alternative to dragging the heavy loads up the paved road.

There wasn't room to drag even one of the four units into the barn with the tractor. We had to remove individual boards on three sides of the barn in order to be able to pull from different directions outside the barn so that we could position the units in such a way that there was room for all of them. Whoever was driving the tractor couldn't see enough through the gap provided by the missing boards and had to rely on the other person stationed inside the barn for stop and go directions. This involved a lot of hooking and unhooking of heavy chains and repositioning the tractor countless times before all four compressors were maneuvered into place.

I think the whole operation took us three days. For some reason, no one was hanging around to watch or lend a hand as so often happened. It was just the three of us: the Ferguson, Dave and me.

Probably because I was less directly involved with it, my recollection of preparing to make the first snow is less clear to me. It was handled by Fred and Ben Blakley and most likely members of their regular crew. It would have involved setting up sections of irrigation pipe (I do recall helping with this part.) and arranging couplings from the power take-off of their big tractor to the drive shaft of the compressor. We used the tractor, probably volunteered by Fred, because the electric service did not have enough power to drive the compressors at that time.

I can remember Ben, huddled on the tractor seat, all bundled up against the cold in overalls and mackinaw, his breath steaming like a teakettle. Insulated clothing not yet being in general use, he was probably wearing several layers underneath the mackinaw which contributed to his almost spherical, gnome-like appearance. Unfortunately, video cameras had not been invented and nobody was taking movies or even still shots of this momentous occasion which seemed like ordinary work at the time. It did draw local spectators, however.

I remember not being favorably impressed with the quality of the snow that was being produced. It was suspiciously like slush that would freeze into ice. Dave was not there for some reason, probably because he had to be at work. I got worried and shut the operation down, probably prematurely, but not before a newly bulldozed area at the bottom of

Brewer Slope had been covered with enough base to make the rest of the snow-covered slope available for skiing that weekend. It may have snowed that night or we may have shoveled snow over that area. In either case, it was deemed a success because skiers were able to cross it with no problem on their way to the tow.

That was the start of snowmaking at Swain as I recall it.

The compressors were subsequently installed in the equipment building below the cliff just to the west of Clark Slope. This must have been after Gunny became outdoor manager because he had built that building from the last stand of hemlock he had managed to cut from a very steep upper slope.[14] The equipment building was not far from our bedroom window. The roar of the machinery had a soporific effect for me, but Dave was always wakeful from concern that the night crew might fall asleep and fail to check that all the nozzles were spewing snow and not (Heaven forbid!) just water, which could happen if an air pipe froze up. Without compressed air to expand it into freezable particles, water would flow from the other pipe and freeze into a river of hard ice.

Dave said he always slept better when son Andy, then a high school student, was a member of the night crew because the snowmobile could be heard going out at more frequent intervals to make sure each nozzle was operating at maximum efficiency. Andy's zeal may have been at least partly due to the opportunity to drive a snowmobile (not otherwise permitted) as to virtuous attention to duty.

---

[14] I was saddened by the loss of the trees which resembled the pillars of a cathedral rising out of the almost vertical slope just below the top of the hill. On more than one occasion, I had taken a break sitting insignificantly beneath their grandeur.

Today, the most sophisticated systems are operated by an employee sitting comfortably at a computer that allows him or her to adjust the air to water ratio for each nozzle, or, in some cases, mostly just sit back and watch a fully automated system operate.

The biggest early improvement to our system was replacing the fit-together sections of aluminum irrigation pipe with welded-together lengths of recycled steel pipe.

At first, it was installed above ground and later reinstalled below ground to help eliminate freeze-ups. At one stage, I remember its being installed during a brutally cold week by a crew from the Pennsylvania oil fields who specialized in pipe installation.

We were constantly making adjustments and trying new techniques and equipment (primarily different types of nozzles), a process that is still probably going on today. Another important development in our day, still in use, was elevating the nozzles on poles or trees so that the mist of snow-forming particles had farther to fall through the cold air and thus more time to crystallize before coming to rest on the ground. I recall Bob James of Kissing Bridge and his outdoor operations manager sharing this idea with us.

My knowledge of subsequent snow-making developments at Swain is scanty. As the area expanded, my attention and energy became concentrated inside the base lodge - on the cafeteria, rental department and ski shop. I do remember that the water supplied by our deep well became insufficient as the system was expanded. We had to run pipe underground from Ewart Creek and, eventually move the pumps and compressors to a new building alongside Canaseraga Creek in order to have enough water.

There is now even a fan jet snowmaker that looks like an airplane engine and eliminates the need for expensive compressed air. It simply spins fast enough to vaporize water coming from numerous apertures without the assistance of compressed air. Another development is SnoMax, a patented chemical that somehow produces greater amounts of snow from the same amount of air, but these developments came after Dave and I had retired.

Daughter Challice recalls snowmaking: as having occurred in two phases: the first experimental and the second, several years later, with rental compressors. "I remember the first year they didn't have residential mufflers and we lived in a cocoon of sound," she writes, "I think this was about 1964."

Snowmaking transformed a very uncertain weather-dependent business (and sport!), especially in the northeastern states to one with a reasonable expectation of being able to continue without intermissions throughout the winter. With the knowledge that they had laid down enough snow to withstand any but the most catastrophic thaw, both ski areas and their customers were able to plan ahead.

Dr. Wende Young, a Rochester physician and member of Hunt Hollow Ski Club, recently told me that she owed her high placements in the United States Ski Association National Senior Races in Montana in 1981 to the fact she had been able to train at Swain during that winter when most western New York areas were closed because of a severe snow drought that year. She came home with trophies for a second place in the downhill and a third place in the giant slalom.

"All other western New York State areas had closed because they didn't have enough base thickness to last through a big thaw in January," she writes. "Swain started early and had enough base to last until mid-March."

From a business standpoint, the more consistent conditions brought about by snowmaking helped to overcome one of the biggest problems of the earliest years: convincing skiers that Swain had good skiing when the ground was bare in Rochester. Ski area snow reports were broadcast on radio stations, and there were numbers to call for the latest report, but people tended to rely on what they could see with their own eyes and didn't bother to call. This was especially true in late March and early April when crocuses and snow drops signaled that spring had arrived even though some of the best skiing of the year was still to be had.

The only disadvantage of snowmaking is its expense. Buying and installing the necessary equipment is major expense, of course, but the heavy cost does not end there. At first glance, it would seem that compressing non-resistant air would be a cinch, but compressing it to the degree needed for making snow requires an enormous amount of power which shows up in electric (or gasoline or diesel) bills.

Ski areas are still a risky, weather-dependent business, but snowmaking has provided more favorable odds albeit at a substantial increase in overhead. Attendance tends to fall off toward the end of the season. Some skiers turn to other activities. Others take a trip to big areas in New England or out West. It is then that operators must weigh the costs of operating at a loss against their responsibility to season pass holders as they watch their costly machine-made snow slowly trickle into neighboring creeks.

Base Lodge

From its exceedingly modest beginning, the base lodge, or Ski Barn as it came to be known locally, went through a series of refinements and additions that transformed it into a comfortable place to warm up, have a meal and socialize. As the number of skiers grew and required more room, the money they brought in enabled us to provide better and more attractive facilities while still keeping a sharp eye on the costs.

Today's structure, which arose after our retirement is positively palatial in comparison. It is nice to know that the old barn with its mortised beams held together with hand-whittled wooden pegs is still there underneath all the improvements, however.

The first improvement to the original room was to lay flooring to replace the rough bark-covered boards in the unused space under the east loft. This expanded the area finished to accommodate customers by 50 percent. Mary's kitchen was moved from its original position under the west loft to this new area alongside the Yencers' yard where the water line from the spring ran past on its way to their house. This enabled Dick Clark to install a big stock-watering tank under the kitchen ceiling providing Mary with what virtually amounted to running water -

at least on temporary basis. At that time, she still had to keep two coffee boilers simmering on the gas burners in order to have hot water, however.

The tank was filled every morning by a hose fed through the kitchen window. It meant that Mary had plenty of water to last throughout the day. It also meant we no longer had to lug milk cans from the spring on the hill.

What a wonderful spring that was! Besides serving four households, it created a swampy area at the foot of the hill that had to be ditched to prevent water from collecting there.[15] The ditch was covered with slab wood from the sawmill and a generous layer of hay. It became a favorite hibernation spot for spotted salamanders, who burrowed holes under the planks. Some were close to an impressive foot in length.

Our need for water grew along with the number of customers. We needed our own supply in order to install inside toilets. John Aronhalt of Nunda drilled a flowing well that tapped a deep underground aquifer. It never went dry even when used as the source of water for snowmaking and now serves the three remaining houses of the four that first shared their water with us.

---

[15] This reminds me of the spring day when the ditch couldn't cope with both the spring overflow and rapidly melting snow. A couple of ski school instructors took advantage of the situation by constructing a small platform of snow that enabled the local kids, and anyone else who wished, to jump over the small pond that accumulated. This went on for an hour or more to everyone's enjoyment, until the instructors, taking advantage of a period when the delighted jumpers were riding up hill for another go, quickly moved the jump fifteen feet or so farther uphill. One by one, the jumpers returned, sailed off the jump and landed in the water. Not realizing the trick that had been played on them, some of the jumpers rode up to try again.

One droughty summer a few years later, when the well that supplied our house failed to produce enough water for toilet flushing, Mary's no-longer-used kitchen storage tank wound up on the porch outside the bathroom. As conditions got even drier, we had to use water from the tank for other purposes as well. That period was later referred to as "the summer we washed the dishes in the toilet-flushing water."

After that summer, we installed a line from the ski area well to our house on "the lane" (which we had bought from Margaret (Underwood) and Norman Didas when they moved to Wayland) and went dry no more. The house has since been demolished along with the century-or-more-old poplar tree that soared above it.

Around this time we were able to improve the ambience in the base lodge by installing a square fireplace open on all four sides in the center of the floor. It had a big metal canopy to carry the smoke up a wide metal chimney. It was constructed by Cleve Dresser of Canaseraga. People could gather round and hang wet mittens on the surrounding guards that kept logs from falling out and people from falling in.

At some point, whether then or during the next expansion, Dave built a long bench with a back across the south side of the room. Sections of the seat lifted up to allow access to the well-seasoned firewood stored there. Much of the wood we burned was bark-backed slab wood, short sections of the strips removed at the sawmill to square logs before they became boards or beams. I enthusiastically rubbed umpteen coats of linseed oil into the finished bench, a big mistake which did not foresee boots, some with metal fittings, being tightened on them, but it was all part of the learning process.

As improvements were made, we were able to create a less austere atmosphere by exposing more of the old barn's supporting beams held together with whittled wooden pegs. We covered the unattractive roofing-covered exterior walls that faced the slopes and parking lot with overlapping planks stained with creosote. The result was a more attractive exterior that was worth the itchy noses and skin rash that appeared after each application of creosote.

Opening up the area under the east loft had a significant personal advantage for Dave and me. Installing a short flight of three steps at one end gave us access to the little loft over what had been a small cow barn attached at a right angle to the main structure. As it could not have sheltered more than a cow or two, their accommodation would have been luxurious in comparison to the crowded conditions most of today's cows endure on today's factory farms.

The steep gambrel roof provided a bit over six feet of head room along about a four-foot wide strip along the middle of the loft above. Along the sides, however, the ceiling was a mere 18 inches or so above the floor, barely enough room to slide a mattress and box spring close to one side and the original kerosene heater from the base lodge as close as we dared get it to the other side. We tacked rolled roofing over the outside and covered it with overlapping boards to match the main barn. Inside, we stapled insulation which, except for the ceiling, we never got around to covering because other things were always more urgent. We didn't dare leave the stove burning when we weren't there, but the small space had the advantage of warming up quickly. It was the height of luxury after sleeping on cold bedding brought in from the car. I don't remember having given any consideration to buying sleeping bags when we were sleeping on the picnic tables, probably because there was never enough money to just go out and buy non-essentials.

During more than one summer, we shared this little abode with a bat who always seemed to have difficulty finding a way out or maybe he was doing us a favor warming up for his nightly foraging trip on an infiltrating mosquito or two that had squeezed through the screens. The bat would flit around and around the small, low-ceilinged room touching the window screening on opposite sides. We would sit up in bed trying to get a look at him only to fall back quickly as he came around again. If there had been anyone to observe the scene it might have looked as if the bat was knocking us down every time he went around. We were never successful in finding him during the day or locating the opening through which he entered and left. Nor did we ever find any droppings so he was not unwelcome as long as he didn't invite any friends.

Somewhere around this time the ground floor of the cow barn served as a rough ski repair shop. Repairs consisted mostly of replacing sections of that time's screwed on edges that had been worn or torn off. I can remember Buster (Duane) Swain doing what needed doing to fix the place up a little and taking care of customers. I can also remember Bill Pierce skillfully making repairs to get skiers back out on the slopes. This was before skis had Teflon bottoms so waxing and even lacquering customers' skis was a constant activity. Bill later ran the improved rental and repair department. His brother Bummy (Bernard) also became involved along with a number of others I can't name at this point. Hollis Baker was in charge at one stage, and LaVerne Wirt and Joe Scott were always a big part of the operation. Everything was a lot more complicated back then when leather boots had to be fitted and laced up. Then, the cable bindings had to be adjusted to fit each individual pair of boots, a far cry today's step-in bindings.

The next addition to the base lodge was the kitchen that was to serve for the rest of our tenure. As for every other building we built, Dave drew up the plans using a skill that he had not previously recognized. This must have been after we were taking in enough money to hire Gunny Yencer as general outdoor manager because we also took advantage of the fact he was a skilled carpenter. I vividly remember planning the inside with him.

It was a good plan that served well except for one thing. For construction details I have since forgotten, Gunny insisted that the main counter should be at the same height as a rather high (about 4 feet) window sill and I couldn't talk him out of it. The result was that the counter was too high for young children and even short adults to pick up their food items easily, but everybody managed with the help of the customers following them. On occasions when no one else was in line, the cashier would get down off her stool and place drinks on the trays. It was all part of the spirit in those less sophisticated days when everybody pitched in to help when needed. I think it was partly due to the attitude of the local community and the surrounding area where people were accustomed to lending a hand where one was needed and partly due the fact that early skiers were exceptionally fine folks, the cream of the crop as it were.

The counter top being at the same level as the window sill tells me that this kitchen which worked so well must have been planned in two stages because it no longer rested on the window sill after it was converted to a U-shaped configuration to encompass a small kitchen for food preparation and allow for a three-compartment sink for washing pots and pans and utensils. The counter retained its original height, however, probably because it covered the steam table hoods and soft drink dispenser. There's much more to tell about the food service so I'll leave it for later and get back to the expansion of the base lodge.

The first major edition was a beauty designed by Dave on the principle of the post and beam construction of his version of a Tech-built house we had built in Honeoye Falls when our expanding family was outgrowing the tenant farm house on Louisa and Eldred Koehler's dairy farm in East Henrietta. When it came time to move to Swain with four pre-school children and run the area full time, one of the hardest things we had to do was leave the first house that was really ours behind. The money from the sale of the house enabled us to get by with no income.

The next addition to the base lodge was a similar building, also designed by Dave with windowed gables and walls overlooking the slopes in two directions. Both additions were built by Bob Perkins, a very satisfactory builder recommended by Bud VanArsdale of the Bank of Castile. This addition, which we called the Shawmut Room, projected beyond the previous one providing shelter from the west wind for a south-facing terrace, which we paved with concrete squares. The old picnic tables, which by then had been succeeded by formica-topped replacements, were moved out onto this space and were very popular on sunny days. The branches of a white pine tree displaced during trail construction spread over the curving concrete steps leading up to the door. We planted evergreen shrubbery next to both buildings with a graceful prunus tree in the corner. We enjoyed being able to provide customers with more than the bare necessities.

The pine tree was so perfect it could have been placed there by a Japanese garden architect. The effect was often enhanced by the presence of a cardinal who frequented the tree and fought with himself in the nearby window. The tree was the only survivor of the three I had once rescued from trail clearance, carried down the hill, one at a time, on a shovel and planted in front of the original outdoor privy. By the time the new addition to the base lodge had stretched out to meet it, the trunk was perhaps a foot in diameter. One of the things that saddened me after Dave and I retired was that the new management ignored my warning that storing salt for the steps over the tree's roots would be harmful. It was. The tree was dead within two years.

The next addition was essentially a vast shed-like addition behind the Shawmut Room to serve the rental department expanding to accommodate the evening school programs Robin Smith successfully introduced after he became head of the ski school. It also provided a picnic area where families could leave picnic baskets on the tables. This left more tables available for cafeteria customers in the other two sections. By this time the ski shop had taken over the entire area provided by the original barn.

That was about the extent of base lodge expansion before we retired. After Robin took over, he built an entirely new two-storey building for the rental department with a picnic room upstairs that also served as headquarters for race management. The old barn was devoted to office space and the concrete floors of the three earlier additions were carpeted over, making them much pleasanter underfoot The old rental department was added onto and became a first class kitchen in which people moved around freely from station to station instead of standing in line - at least until they reached the cashier. This progress, plus a further large two-storey addition with a formal restaurant upstairs, was to come a steep price, but more on that later.

The Cafeteria Crew

The earliest days when Mary Clark coped with primitive conditions such as a limited supply of water and having to lug supplies from her home in Irondequoit near Rochester, are described beginning in the earlier chapter of my somewhat random recollections. I can't remember seeing her in the improved kitchen with infinitely running water afforded by the first addition to the original barn, but Challice recalls her working there with daughter Gail sometimes helping. I can't even remember who ran the old kitchen the year after Dick died for that matter but it seems Canaseraga stalwarts Vivian Baker and Grace Klos must have absorbed much of the load as the primary responsibility for the food service fell into my already too busy hands.

My earliest recollection after I had to take over is of washing coffee mugs whenever a lull in ski shop business allowed me to do so. (It was handy that the ski shop was across an open corridor from the kitchen making it easier to assess where I could be most effective.) The mugs had a way of accumulating rapidly in one of a pair of deep sinks during the busiest times when nobody could take time to wash them because they were too busy serving customers. While performing this useful chore, I could observe what was going on and consider making changes that would improve food quality and service.

This happened around the time Styrofoam cups were becoming available. Partly out of concern for the contribution of disposables to the trash mountains rising in the environment, but also because of distaste for the flavor the paper cups of those days imparted to hot drinks, we had stuck with the mugs. Cost may also have been a factor, but the combination of taste-free disposable cups, convenience, labor reduction, and the need for more storage space to help us accommodate enough mugs for the rapidly growing number of customers overcame environmental scruples. At this point I can only wonder what became of all those old thick white ceramic mugs and the newer more glass-like green and beige ones.

Cold drinks were served in the red and white paper cups available from the Dansville Coca Cola® distributor. I wonder now if whoever was the boss at Coca Cola® appreciated the hard work performed by Art Morsch to get their product to its destination at Swain. At first it was heavy wooden crates of glass bottles and later pressurized containers which had to be hooked up to a dispenser. I can remember Art, always cheerful, pulling a hand truck through unplowed snow and up steps to make the delivery - on Thursdays, I think it was.

The most popular food items were hamburgers and hot dogs. On busy days, Vivian and Grace worked constantly to keep the grill loaded, rolls warmed and customers served with steam table items like soup, chili and hot chocolate. Vivian, who claimed to have asbestos fingers, had had a lot of experience with church suppers and other events that involved feeding a lot of people. Swain residents, Leila Pierce and Joanne Carpenter, Esther Dieter, Lucille Tucker and Lula Griffith were long-time regulars. Del Neary, Bonnie Saunders and Ruth Smith of Canaseraga were also part of the crew for many years in addition to Vivian and Grace from that village.

The cash register required someone who could quickly add up a trayfull of items in her head. This was facilitated by having prices rounded off by fives and tens, no 49 or 98-cent items. When sales tax became a factor, we included it in the price of each item and paid the county a percentage of the gross. With a nimble-brained cashier on duty, this system was actually faster than some of the more elaborate ones in use today, which require waiting for the machine to do its stuff. I particularly remember Barb and Ted Swain and Loretta Ames ably performing this critical function which took disciplined concentration in the midst of a lot of bustle.

Outside of peak periods, the crew was free to take turns taking breaks to sit down in the dining room when the all the work was caught up. I didn't notice them doing this very much, however, and they certainly didn't abuse the privilege. It seemed that they preferred to remain standing behind the counter during slack periods, catching up on each other's news. Sometimes, they changed positions during slack periods for the novelty of it. On really slow days, they undertook on their own initiative jobs like cleaning refrigerator shelves and straightening up the adjacent storeroom.

The crew was really pretty much autonomous. All I had to do was keep them supplied and post a schedule of who was working when. Making changes to the schedule for personal needs, such as a family birthday or attending a friend's wedding, could get complicated and consume as much as half an hour of time I couldn't afford to lose until I suggested that they arrange for their own substitutes. This worked like a charm as there was usually somebody glad to swap or take on extra hours.

Then, there were the times when we were overstaffed because business was slower than I had anticipated. Sometimes on these occasions, a crew member would come up to me suggesting that she go home where there was more to do if I didn't feel she was really needed. This saved her from a boring day of standing around waiting for customers and saved the area from having to pay her for doing so.

I suppose the prevailing good work ethic was due to the influence of small family farms where everybody just naturally pitched in because there was so much work to be done. I remember one girl whose name won't come to me, a product of a farm west of Dalton coming back to thank me for my letter of recommendation in connection with her application for joining one of the armed services The recruiter had shown her the letter which was deservedly very commendatory. "I never knew I did all of those things!" she said. My point is that it was just second nature for most area people and an important factor in the area's success.

One of the biggest and mostly unseen contributors worked in our house, just a few steps from the base lodge. Eunice Gaby's first job was to look after our four children on weekends when Dave and I were fairly leaping to fill one need after another with no time to listen properly and respond to the needs of our children. The children were 1, 2, 3, and 4 at the time we moved to Swain to start full-time operation, but Eunice, who had taught in the one-room Klipnocky district school, managed well and was able to keep the cafeteria supplied with our own specially-made hot chocolate at the same time.

The usual thing in commercial operations at that time was to add hot water to the contents of a packet of dry ingredients in each cup. Besides being too slow to prepare for each customer, the results couldn't hold a candle to the real thing. So, we made our own which tasted better and could be quickly ladled out of a steam table well.

It was some time after I took over from Mary Clark before we had a supplier who could furnish us with hamburger patties so Eunice made these too, using an ice cream scoop and pressing them between two sheets of waxed paper. The children were older by then and sometimes helped her with this when they weren't out skiing.

As you would expect, hot foods were always in demand, but there was also a demand for regular sandwiches - especially as the weather warmed in March and April - and no room to make them in the base lodge before an addition was made to the cafeteria. My cutting board at the time, and still in use, was the irregular end of a foot-wide pine board. It nicely held four slices of bread. Eunice used it to make and wrap four sandwiches at a time: tuna salad, egg salad, and a particularly unhealthy, but popular, combination of ham and sour cream. When Eunice was no longer available to work after she started to provide residential care for senior citizens in her home, her daughter Jean Wirt, wife of LaVerne, a pillar of the early ski shop and rental department, took over the job of keeping the cafeteria supplied.

The door to our house was just a few steps from the base lodge, but it required a "runner" to ferry supplies back and forth. I can remember Susie Blakley, daughter of Ron and Dolores (who worked in the ski shop, did payroll and helped with bookkeeping), and Beverly Tucker, Allegany County Dairy Princess and daughter of Lois and Vincent who farmed at the head of the valley, ably ferrying supplies back and forth in between cleaning trays and wiping tables.

The runner's job was eliminated by an addition to the cafeteria which included a cold room as well as more refrigeration and storage space for supplies. The big change, however, was a "country kitchen" which converted the cafeteria line from a single straight line to three sides of a rectangle. The new kitchen, capably manned by Lucille Tucker, enabled us to offer more variety as well as to eliminate all the running back and forth between our office/residence and the base lodge. Lucille brought her own electric fryer in which she made fresh donuts early on weekend mornings. The donuts were top notch and disappeared as fast as they made it to the counter top.

In the new kitchen, a regular household stove with an oven enabled Lucille to make batch after batch of chocolate cupcakes using our family recipe for "Auntie Betty's Chocolate Cake." [16] Nowadays, because the recipe requires neither milk nor eggs, it keeps appearing under various names in vegan and vegetarian cookbooks. Our copy, well spotted with chocolate batter, is written in green ink to match the leaves and stems of a big red rose on a piece of lined stationary, the gift of a young child to her teacher, my sister. I think we increased the amount of cocoa which made them very chocolatey despite their very light texture.

In spite of the fact there still wasn't much room to work, Lucille took over the sandwich making and the hot chocolate making that Eunice had done while looking after our children. She also took over my job of making chili from scratch. There wasn't a recipe for it until Lucille wrote one down as we worked together on a couple of batches. I don't

---

[16] Recipe for Auntie Betty's Chocolate Cake: Mix together 1 ½ cups sifted flour, 4 T cocoa, 1 t baking soda, 1 cup sugar, ½ t salt. Add 5 T oil, 1 T vinegar, 1 t vanilla, and 1 cup water. Beat until smooth. Pour into 9 X 9 pan and bake at 350 for 30 minutes. (Jeanie always doubles the cocoa.)

remember it now except that it had lots of onions and three kinds of fresh peppers and was very popular.[17]

I think the occasion for Lucille taking over the chili making was the time I fell asleep on my feet leaning against a door frame while waiting for the ground beef to brown between stirrings. I awoke with a start to see a black cloud emerging from the kettle - the implausible kind of cloud sometimes depicted in cartoons - and making its way across the kitchen and into the living room.

My recollection is that I used to start each batch with 50 pounds of ground beef which in this case all had to be discarded. Worse yet, the expensive stainless steel kettle had begun to melt, disfiguring its flat bottom with what looked like a steel icicle. In spite of running the evacuation fan for what was left of the night, the house harbored the horrible odor for several days. This minor setback in the whole scheme of things, sticks in my mind, mostly because it's the only time I ever remember falling asleep on my feet. The steel icicle was ground flat and for all I know that big kettle is still in use.

We experimented with the menu by offering tossed "super" salads and even a regular meal at noon on weekdays, but most of our customers stated their preference by continuing to order the familiar hots, hamburgers and chili.

Weather forecasting being less accurate back then, it was all but impossible to predict on what day the season would end. The hamburgers arrived

---

[17] After we had retired and had time to think about what we were eating, Dave took up cooking and concocted an even tastier all-veggie recipe, which won first place in a vegetarian cooking contest.

frozen anyway and could be kept that way for the next season, but rolls presented a problem because they required more freezer space than we had to accommodate them. Money always being a primary concern, rather than throwing them out, I sliced them into thin slices and converted them into French toast for family breakfasts.

One year we lost the entire contents of an ice cream freezer packed full with hamburger because someone coming in to fix a furnace had unplugged the freezer in order to use an extension cord and then neglected to plug it in again. The loss was aggravated by the fact that I had to unload the rotten slimy mess and clean, disinfect and air the inside of the box-like freezer several times to make sure no trace of spoilage remained. I managed to do this without vomiting by pulling my shirt over my nose and breathing through my mouth so I couldn't smell what must have been a terrible stench.

Then there was the matter of Allegany County's hiring a restaurant health inspector who insisted that we had to install a three-compartment sink in order to be in compliance with the law. By this time we were using disposable dishes and silverware so the third sink which was to be used for sanitizing, i.e. disinfecting, dishes, was of marginal use. We bought the largest sink that the space would accommodate but were still faced with the problem of washing our largest cooking pots which did not fit into the smaller compartments of the new sink, but that was apparently of less concern to the inspector than complying with the law. The insides of the pots were no problem, of course, and we just did the best we could with the outsides while balancing the pots on the edge of the sink.

After this, I didn't go out of my way to welcome the inspector's monthly visits, especially when I was busy in the ski shop. Instead, I inflicted him on poor Dave who had developed a good relationship with our more affable[18] lift inspector and was resigned to wasting time just chatting for a couple of hours. Dave had a way of agreeing with someone proposing changes and then doing as he thought best or, in this case, giving me the room to do so.

After we started full 7-day operation, my days began at 6 a.m. when I poured buckets of water into the steam table and lit its two gas burners so that it would be warmed up when it was time to start loading it at 8:00 a.m. Unlike the steam table, the coffee urn had water piped in so all I had to do to fill its surrounding jacket was to open the valve. The only problem was that it did not shut off automatically when full. On more than one occasion, it overflowed while I was filling the steam table or getting supplies from the freezer. Wonderful start for the day! Worse yet, there were at least a couple of occasions when it overflowed while customers were being served. I doubt that it is still in use anywhere.

At the height of the season, it was a rare Saturday night when I didn't have to drive the family station wagon to Hornell to replenish supplies. Daughter Jeanie who had been instructing and skiing all day often accompanied me, which was a big help both physically and psychologically. We would typically fill five grocery carts with everything from fresh vegetables to candy bars and other supplies. In addition there would be five or six cases of oranges and apples. We sold the fruit for a quarter, which seemed too expensive to me until I saw it being sold for fifty cents at other areas.

---

[18] The lift inspector's affability may have had something to do with the fact that when Bill Jenkins was outdoor manager, he would get teenaged Jeanie to sit and talk with him "to make him more agreeable."

Steve Panogataga, the manager of Wegman's store in Hornell and his staff were very helpful, bringing fruit from their storage area and loading everything in the station wagon for us. One Christmas Eve, Steve showed up at our house with his family and a load of fruit that had not been available on my last visit to his store. He was so enthusiastic about fruit that I had originally thought him to be the produce manager rather than Wegman's Hornell head honcho. He worked with me to supply apples other than the red delicious, which have so bland in flavor that I have always deemed them unworthy to be called apples, but our customers voted with their eyes and went for the shiny red delicious variety 95% of the time.

It was always a relief to have the shopping accomplished but it still had to be unloaded when we got back after being careful to ease the loaded station wagon across the railroad tracks so that its bottom didn't scrape on the rails. Lucille's children, Paul, Kevin, and especially Karen were a big help with this. The lifts would have shut down and they would be waiting for Lucille to finish work and drive home to their farm at the head of the valley. I particularly remember how adept Karen, who was only eight or nine at the time, was at knowing which bag to relieve you of when you were carrying too many. She was later to become an efficient member of the cafeteria crew.

After we started 7-day and night operation, everything had to be cleaned and mopped every night with most of the crew staying on to do so. Before that time, we had left thorough cleaning until Monday morning. Esther Dieter, Joanne Carpenter and Lucille Tucker most regularly performed this chore. They made sort of a social occasion of it carrying on a conversation by calling back and forth to each other from different rooms without letting up on their efforts to mop and scrub everything in sight. Dave often remarked on their ability to do this after his work had required a trip to the base lodge from the office in our house. Daughter Challice remembers once begging Lucille's niece, Beverly Tucker, to let her start sweeping because it seemed like so much fun. Challice had been helping the night before when everybody was singing "Down in the Valley" as they worked.

The area was fortunate to have such a jolly, hard-working crew, chattering amongst themselves when they weren't busy serving customers. At times it seemed as if they were volunteers working together on a church supper or some similar mutual endeavor. Of course there were minor dissatisfactions and differences of opinion at times, but they got sorted out one way or another and team spirit prevailed. Looking back, I'm not sure I realized at the time how fortunate we were to have such a hard-working, cooperative staff.

The Swain Ski Patrol

One of the strongest attributes of Swain has always been the high caliber of its ski patrol. In the beginning, it was just Dick Clark, Dave and me with Dick, as patrol leader, shouldering the heaviest share of the burden. This was partly because of his training and experience as a scout leader and partly because he was less bogged down in business details and more likely to be out on the slopes when a patroller was needed. I remember all three of us attending evening first aid classes in Rochester.

Dick brought in fellow scout master Ray Meyering who was also a New York State Trooper and used to dealing with accidents. Members of the Powder Patrol of Pittsford who served Powder Mill Park including Dwight Hill, Al Yole, Charlie Edwards and Don Greenfield were very helpful and supportive as visiting patrollers in the early years. Early Swain Patrollers included Don Seitz, Cliff Champion, Ernie Neben and Dick Tardiff. Marty Kron was a stalwart member for years, as were Bill Murphy and Judy and John Sherman until they moved to New England.

The two senior members of the Swain Patrol for years were Herbie Lehman and Harry Stoneham. Harry served as patrol leader for eight years during the sixties. With 53 years of service as a patroller, Harry was finally forced to retire in 2005 due to physical problems. Herb is still patrolling actively and continues to assist in training skiing and toboggan handling. He is one of the longest serving patrollers in the country, having served for over 60 years! Terry Smith, who joined the Swain Patrol in 1972, is still an active patroller and is our senior woman on the patrol.

Dave and I became inactive as these and other capable and conscientious people took over and ran a very professional patrol with no remuneration other than the satisfaction of helping fellow skiers.

The first patrol room was a rough one, just a third of the ground floor under one of the lofts in what had been John Brewer's barn. If there was a window, it was a small one because the room was dark and uninviting except for the fact it was heated.

The "toboggan" for transporting injured skiers consisted of a stretcher mounted on a pair of sturdy seven-foot army skis, the kind issued to troops of the 10th Mountain Division in World War II. The stretcher was equipped with a plywood back board to be used in case of back injury, a Thomas splint for broken legs, and of course some blankets. Dick Clark took the lead in getting these bare necessities together, some of which were almost surely donated by well-wishers.

The poverty of these early facilities was compensated for by the quality of patrol members and the luxury of having doctors who liked to ski as honorary patrol members. It was reassuring for all concerned, not least the victims of more serious injuries, to have them look in when something out of the ordinary occurred. I think Jim McFarland, a radiologist from nearby Hornell, was the first. In the early days before there was night skiing, he and his wife Annette even went out of their way to entertain patrollers and local skiers at parties in their home.

Betty and Allan Harder, both MDs, began to practice in Hornell early on and someone introduced Marian and George Emerson, also both MDs as well as skiers, who practiced in Rochester about the same time. There were others as well, but these five kept coming back for a couple of decades or more sharing their knowledge for the benefit of their fellow man and helping to make it possible for the area to get on with its job of providing skiing for people in the area. This association started back before our national litigiousness drove doctors' insurance rates over the moon, but these friends continued to serve their fellow skiers.

Dr Anne Harrison, a pediatrician from Scottsville, was an active member of the patrol for many years. She served evening shifts when there was an increased injury load due to the school groups.

The next patrol room was a step up. Viola and Dick Blowers and daughters Patty, Bonnie, Mary Lou and son Jim, who had been temporarily living in a small house up against the steep bank at the base of the hill, moved to a more substantial house in the center of town. Their erstwhile house, known after a former occupant as the "Riley Elster House," remained vacant and appeared on the tax sale roll the following summer. I remember going by myself to Belmont to bid on it. We were the only ones interested in it, but the county had a real estate agent bidding on it until the bid reached some pre-determined level it considered reasonable. I kept raising the bid by just ten dollars or so until the agent stopped bidding and we had acquired a critical piece of property, not so much the house itself, but the small plot of land surrounding it, which later provided valley-floor access between the north and east-facing slopes.

The downstairs consisted of two small rooms, but they were light and bright and cheerful compared to the gloomy old room in the Brewer barn. The ski patrol eagerly took over and, doing the work themselves, converted them to suit their needs. Having a second storey over the small ground floor made the house seem disproportionately tall. Covering the outside with boards and battens gave it an appealing American gothic aspect, but the improvements were mostly designed to facilitate the handling of injured skiers. A ramp allowed toboggans to be slid up onto the porch and into one of the rooms.

Over the years, equipment was constantly being upgraded indoors and out. New patrollers were being trained and certified to serve at other areas as well as Swain and it was all accomplished autonomously by the patrol members. Instead of the hand-cranked phones and skier-delivered messages of those days, each patroller now wears an FM radio tied to the patrol base station so that everyone is in touch with what is going on and able to make decisions such as who is in the best position to respond most quickly to a reported accident. The Patrol grew to over 100 members to assure that all seven-day and seven-night shifts could be adequately staffed. And the entire Swain Patrol is staffed with unpaid volunteers, a unique situation in the industry today!

Today the greatly expanded group continues to provide Good Samaritan services for those in need. It does so from a more spacious and vastly improved building, constructed in 1978 by the volunteer labor of the patrollers with materials provided by the ski center. There is even a proper office for the patrol leader upstairs in addition to a kitchen, picnic tables and luxurious sofas donated by patrol members. The sofas can even be slept on if a patroller needs to stay overnight to meet the next day's schedule. Each member has a cubby hole to hold his boots and a smaller item or two. But this is again beyond the period of which I am writing. I just don't want to leave the reader with the impression that the Swain Ski Patrol is still in what some might consider the dark ages while others look back fondly on "the good old days" as they enjoy the comforts of today.

SWAIN SKI PATROL LEADERS

Richard Clark *	1947 - 1958
Glenn Austin *	1958 - 1961
Harry Stoneham	1961 - 1969
William McKenna *	1969 - 1971
James Ebmeyer	1971 - 1975
Ernest Brown	1975 - 1979
Bert Sliker **	1979 - 1980
Ted Snyder	1980 - 1985
Robert Melville	1985 - 1987
Merle Eldridge	1987 - 1991
Jeanne Eldridge	1991 - 1995
Ted Snyder	1995 - 1997
Myron Crispino	1997 - 2001
Joseph Menichino	2001 - 2005
Tim Cassidy	2005 -

* deceased
** Bert resigned as Patrol Leader after one year to become Section Chief of the Genesee Valley Section.

Swain Ski School

There wasn't any ski school per se to begin with. It was just me sharing my experience with the local children and the occasional customer who needed to learn the rudiments of sidestepping uphill and snowplowing to control speed on the way back down.

It wasn't long before an experienced instructor found us, however. Vermont native Ralph Plumb, who worked with patients at the Bath Veterans' Hospital, came to ski. When we learned that he had taught at Ascutney Mountain in southern Vermont, we asked if he would consider teaching at Swain, which he did until he was transferred to a different VA center. He may have done all the instructing himself because I don't recall his having had a staff. I do remember, however, that his graceful skiing attracted everyone's attention and that he was a favorite of staff in the base lodge who appreciated his modest gentlemanly manner.

Bill DeWolfe followed Ralph and trained a staff of instructors to meet the needs of the growing number of skiers. The first time I met Bill was in 1940. He was working during the winter as a salesman and ski technician for Ruby Gordon Sporting Goods, which I believe was then Rochester's only ski shop. I remember having difficulty finding Ruby's store because I was new to Rochester and didn't realize that street names changed after they crossed Main Street. I couldn't find South Avenue because I was walking up and down on the north side of Main where what was apparently the same street was named St. Paul, all the time carrying a ski badly in need of repair in a busy shopping area.

Bill expertly sawed out the damaged section of hickory near the tip of the ski, replaced it with a sound piece of wood and installed a new section of edge, which meant I would be able to ski again the next time it snowed.

Shortly after that, our country became more actively involved in World War II. I didn't know until later that Bill had become a ski instructor for the 10th Mountain Division which served so well in the Italian Alps. Nor did I know until later that he had built a large log cabin, installed a rope tow, and started a private ski club on land he rented from a farmer in the Bristol Hills. I don't remember whether it was his idea or ours that he should take over our ski school after Ralph was transferred outside our area.

At any rate, Bill trained a staff of perhaps a dozen (many more over the long run) instructors, including his wife Helen. In addition to helping a lot of people become skiers, the ski school staff added much interest to the Saturday night après ski scene.

When the area swung from a weekend operation to seven/day, seven/night schedule, Robin Smith took over as ski school director bringing with him Chic Carlucci as assistant director. By this time, or not long after, Robin resigned from his teaching position at Letchworth Central School in order to devote full time to the ski school and area promotion.

Chic, on the other hand, went on to become assistant principal. After Robin left, Chic took over as ski school director and remained in that position for a decade after he had retired from Letchworth in 1994. He now resides for the winter in Park City, Utah with his wife Joan, also a former certified Swain instructor. They ski over 100 days each year.

After Robin first took over, he engaged two former pupils from the Castile area to handle lessons on midweek days: Glenn Lapham and David Wagenblass. David was nicknamed "Wheels," not because he a flashy show-off but as word play on "wagon wheels." They were both nice young men, on the conservative side, but delighted to have found a job that paid them for helping others to enjoy the sport they loved.

It was not to last, however. When it seemed that they were really sitting in the catbird seat, both tragically died on their way to a celebratory dinner in an automobile accident on the horseshoe bend on the back road between Canaseraga and Arkport. I don't believe the cause of the accident was ever ascertained, but there was speculation that a tractor's rear-facing lights could have been mistaken for headlights. Dave was not at all the type to drive too fast. Suffice it to say, Dave's car was a small Volkswagen beetle that offered little protection to its passengers. Both were pronounced dead at the scene.

Everyone was devastated at the loss of these promising young men. That's why two side-by-side trails bear the names of Glenn's Run and Wheels' Run.

Robin was nationally known as a member of the National Ski Instructors Association's elite demo team. When he and Chic first took over the ski school, it had 12 instructors. When Chic retired as director in 2004, the staff had grown to 120 instructors. Before the cost of transportation became what it is today, the instructors taught approximately 20,000 students per season. Today, I'm told the numbers have dropped to approximately 6,000 students.

The ski school generated a lot of business for the area by instigating and administering specially-priced ski programs for students in area schools. The package included lessons and lift tickets with the option of adding equipment rental. The schools furnished chaperones who received the same benefits free of charge for handling attendance and financial details.

The price sometimes seemed absurdly low, but the program generated skiers who would be buying lift tickets for years to come and even persuaded parents to take up the sport instead of just watching their kids have all the fun. Skiing brightened the lives of hundreds, or more likely thousands, of area people by giving them something to look forward to in the winter months. Much of the success of the program was attributable to the administration of Robin's wife, Sharon Bailey.

Chic informs me several alumni of the ski school went on to carve out successful careers in the ski industry. Tim Petrick, who stayed on for a while as an instructor, became the President of the K2 Ski Company. Tim often stayed overnight with the Carluccis' and babysat their children Brian and Karen.

Diann Roffe, who became an Olympic gold medalist, learned to ski at Swain while her father, Bob Roffe was an instructor there. Bob was later associated with Brantling Hill, a ski area north of Rochester so Diann came to be associated with Brantling rather than with Swain.

AJ Kitt, whose parents Nancy and Ross were both Swain instructors, went on to become a downhiller on the U.S. Olympic Team. He competed in a record four Olympic meets around the world and captured several World Cup medals.

The ski school managed races for the schools in New York State's Section Five as well as for various ski club meets. They also ran Nastar races on Wednesdays for anyone who wanted to don a bib and run the course for practice or just for fun. They also conducted special classes in racing as well as a special racing program during the Christmas holidays.

Several metropolitan ski clubs from the Cleveland Ohio area have held an annual meet at Swain for over a couple of decades. Daughter Challice became an out-of-state member of one of the clubs and races on their team.

Joan Carlucci, who was also a certified instructor, reminds me that she and Chic were instrumental in forming the Swain Ski Club so that skiers interested in racing could participate in races sanctioned by the Eastern Ski Association. She remembers timing racers with Bob Miller in his van, a very cold job at times.

Bob was the patriarch of the Miller family who comprised a significant part of the ski school for decades. His wife Lu and their children, Judy, Tom, Kris, Dave and Andrea instructed for many years, while Bob performed many useful chores in support. Kris organized a program called SkiWee (later called Ski Zoo) designed for very young children to have fun while learning.

Before racing became more popular and took precedence, the ski school taught special classes in "freestyle" skiing, a combination of graceful ballet and acrobatics still on the list of national and international competitive events. It has become more breathtakingly acrobatic over time. The area even had its own demo team comprised of young area skiers who performed spectacular maneuvers in unison. Conventional skiers were entertained while riding up the lift by seeing demo team members performing sweeping arabesques across the slopes or aerial 360's as the spirit moved them. Today, it is more likely to be the snow boarders who go in for extraordinary stunts although a few intrepid skiers make use of the special terrain park created to give boarders more opportunities to get airborne and perform aerial feats.

The area (and its customers) has been fortunate in having high quality instructors dedicated to using their skills and knowledge to help others learn and hone their skills to achieve maximum enjoyment.

The Swain Ski Shop and Rental Department

We had never planned to run a ski shop. It was one of those things that just happened in the course of providing for our customers' needs. I think the first item we carried was the Bousquet rope tow gripper, which sold for $3.

The grippers were sold out of ticket window at the base of the main tow. As I often filled this position in the earliest days, I acquired knowledge of skiers' needs first hand. It wasn't long before we added a couple of shelves in the booth to hold boot laces, goggles, ski waxes, lip salve, sun lotion and packets of tissues.

Skiers' requests also led to a bottle of aspirin tablets being kept with these other items. There was no charge for these. We just had the person hold out a hand and shook a couple of tablets into it as we continued to do for the next 30 years.

Eventually, there being no ski shops within a 50-mile radius at the time, we advanced to skis, boots and clothing, but that was after the ski shop was moved into the base lodge and became an enterprise in itself. In the meantime, to meet the occasional demand for rental equipment, the ticket booth was replaced by a small building with the ticket window at one end.

Our neighbor Alton Spencer, a carpenter who lived with his wife Herthel and children (Peggy, Linda, Peter and Susie) next to the western corner of the area, spent a week's vacation building a new combination ticket booth and space to hold a few pairs of rental skis. It had two big multi-paned windows on the south side. These were left over from the first phase of base lodge. It was seldom that any material went to waste.

When ticket sales, rentals and what merchandise we had were moved to the base lodge, this attractive little building became headquarters for the ski school, directed at the time by 10th Mountain Division veteran, Bill DeWolfe. I never knew until just recently what happened to this little building after the ski school got a more capacious building to suit its expanding needs.

When the building was doomed to be burned to get it out of the way, Harry Weaver asked if he could draw it away instead. He and Lyle mounted it on skids and hauled it to land Harry had acquired up the valley, much the way Dave and I had handled the snowmaking compressors. The size of the building made theirs a much more formidable operation as they had to maneuver it around countless curves as they followed the narrow road up the valley. It was nice to learn that it is now situated overlooking a stream and still in use for camping and family gatherings.

After moving into early base lodge, the shop took over the alcove under the east loft next to the kitchen. After new additions were added for the kitchen and the first big dining area, the ski shop expanded to take over the entire first floor of the original barn and eventually, after the addition of two more dining areas, part of the original dining addition.

The rental equipment, though new, was not of the best, but it helped a few people get a taste of the sport and decide whether or not to take it up. In retrospect, it was more likely to discourage all but the most enthusiastic from doing so, but so was the equipment most people were using. Skis had screwed-on edges and cable bindings to hold boots in a toe bracket. A leather strap across the toe kept the boot from popping out.

As business increased, rentals became separate from the ski shop, with repairs, headed by Joe Scott[19] and LaVerne Wirt[20] of Canaseraga, handling both needs. Joe and LaVerne did the critical work of accurately mounting and adjusting bindings to customers' skis and boots for a couple of decades or so. As their work load increased, we had to hire others to relieve them of rental concerns and help with other shop work as well. Both drove big semis for Shay's Trucking of Dansville during

---

[19] Joe's wife, Norma, was part of the cafeteria crew. Their daughter Joette also worked with her mom from time to time. To my recollection son John did not work at the area, but he was an excellent skier. - Jeanie

[20] LaVerne was married to Eunice Gaby's daughter Jean who took over her mother's job of keeping the cafeteria supplied from our kitchen before base lodge had one of its own. Daughter Challice recalls one New Year's Day when Joe and LaVerne both had severe headaches. Convinced by a major thaw and a huge sheet of standing water in Canaseraga on December 31 that there would be no skiing the next day, they felt free to celebrate well into the morning hours. It is to their credit that they showed up instead of sleeping in as they had anticipated.

the day, and I know there were times in the early days when they would have preferred to stay home after dinner rather than go back out to mount bindings.

I can't begin to remember all the people who worked in the rental department. The first I recall were Duane ("Buster") Swain and Bill Pierce making the best of crude conditions in the basement of the cow barn. They were followed by Hollis Baker,[21] and, at a later date, Bill's brothers Bernard ("Bummy") and Dennis (sons of Leila, a mainstay of the cafeteria, and Bill Pierce who lived up the valley), Dave Hedden, Fran Coombs, LaRue ("Butch") Underwood, Donny Johnson and Nate Myers. Danny ("Moon") Rawleigh also comes to mind.

Everything was a lot more complicated back then when leather boots had to be fitted and laced up. Then, the cable bindings had to be adjusted to fit each individual pair of boots, a far cry today's step-in bindings.

The 20th century saw a lot of changes in ski equipment. The earliest bindings were designed to do one thing: bond the boot with the ski. The very earliest ones, consisting of a leather toe strap and another leather strap around the heel, didn't even do that very well. The next step was to incorporate into the leather strap a steel spring to fit around the heel to give more flexibility. Bootmakers responded by producing boots with a groove to help hold the spring in place. The leather part tended

---

[21] Hollis had his own carpentry and plumbing business and did a lot of work for us and everybody else. His wife Vivian was a mainstay of the cafeteria and their daughter Sheila and sons Steve, Phillip ("Buzzy"), Maurice ("Moe") and Bill worked in rentals and as lift attendants. I was planning to consult Hollis a couple of weeks ago, but had instead to attend his farewell visiting hours.

to stretch on warm days making it necessary to move the buckle to the next hole in the strap as you would tighten a belt.

To obtain an even closer bond with the ski, some elite skiers used long thongs, long leather straps which wrapped around the boots several times and lashed them firmly to D-rings on the skis. The thongs also served to beef up the meager support afforded by the boots of those days. Neither thongs nor early cables had any release capability in case of a fall. They were designed to do one thing: bond the boot with the ski. Needless to say, the injury rate was proportionately, but not numerically, higher.

By the time Swain got underway, the leather heel straps had been replaced by steel cables with heel springs, but leather toe straps were still pretty normal. The all-metal cables were a big improvement but prone to developing kinks where they were held down by hooks on the sides of the skis.

Adjusting the cables to fit different boot sizes was a miserable job. The coarse adjustment using notches on the lever that snugged the cable up to the boot was straightforward enough, but the final adjustment that involved turning the hollow nuts on either side of the heel spring involved a lot of fiddling around. The worst of it was that there was no indication of how much cable lay hidden under the nut. When there wasn't enough, it fell apart and necessitated moving the cable to a different notch and starting the final adjustment all over again.

Eventually bindings were developed with boot attachments that allowed every boot to fit every ski without any fiddling around, a development that made the old cable adjustments seem like something out of the dark ages. I think Spademan was one of the first to do so by using a large metal plate on the sole of each boot.

Before cables became extinct, manufacturers developed a number of toe pieces that swiveled to either side when subjected to too much pressure by a falling skier. They undoubtedly prevented some sprains and broken bones but couldn't hold a candle to the more sophisticated bindings yet to come.

Mitch Cubberly (Cubco) in New Jersey and Earl Miller in Utah improved the connection between boot and binding by using metal plates on the boots to assure a precise connection while providing release capability in multiple directions. Their innovative bindings gradually saw less use, however, as the development of more rigid boots allowed bindings to be engineered with ever improving release mechanisms.

Other manufacturers developed heel and toe pieces that provided increasingly secure connections combined with increasingly improved release capabilities. Collaboration between boot and binding manufacturers resulted in bindings becoming ever more sophisticated (and more expensive) pieces of machinery, a far cry from the simple leather heel and toe straps and even farther from the slice of old automobile inner tube I can remember using to perform this function as a child.

The first boots were not much better than a stiff work shoe with a square toe to fit the toe bracket mounted on the ski. Then came "double boots" with an inner boot to hold the foot more firmly and give the skier a little better control. Sometime - in the late 50's, I think it was - someone thought of using buckles with adjustable notches to provide leverage for closing the increasingly stiffer leather boots. We first became aware of this development in boots from Henke, a Swiss boot-making firm we dealt with.

Even though buckle boots were considerably more expensive than the lace ones that were in general use, we personally took advantage of this development so that our pre-school children could put their boots on by themselves.

Lace and the early buckle boots still made of leather took a lot of fitting and we earned a reputation for being good at it. We learned what had to be done by listening to our customers, making adjustments and encouraging them to spend time walking around in their selection to give trouble spots a chance to develop. By we, I mean besides myself people like Barb Swain, Dolores Blakley, Dave Hedden and Terry Johnson who listened and acted upon what the customer being fitted told them.

Laces were hard on the boot-fitter's hands, particularly the outer side of the little finger, which was likely to develop a raw groove where the laces dug in as they were tightened. I still have a pair of unlined leather driving gloves given to me by Joey Long, a sympathetic friend and customer whose husband David was our insurance agent.

With no way of pressing the unyielding toes of children's boots to judge the right size, we had them, and adult customers as well, slide a foot forward until the toes touched the front of the boot. We could then judge the correct length by sliding our fingers down the inside of the back of the boot to see how much space there was behind the heel. One finger width was usually right for adults. Two fingers behind a child's heel gave the likelihood that, barring an unusual winter growth spurt, the boot would fit for two years. Nowadays, with hard shell boots and more people skiing, shops are able to offer to rent boots for the season with the opportunity to move up a size if a child's foot should grow during the winter.

We had a press that enabled us to give closer fits to provide better control by reshaping the boot to create a little more space around a sensitive bone or joint. This process often required spending hours at a time with a customer. This became unnecessary as boots evolved into sort of a standard container with inside adjustments enabling it to be fitted to the various shapes and sizes of individual feet. I think Rosemonts were the first of this type of custom-fitted boot. They were also a forerunner in the trend to use synthetic materials instead of leather. This type of boot had the advantage for the shop of not having to stock so many different sizes.

At one stage of boot development, manufacturers came up with the idea of injecting a special inner compartment with a chemical that expanded into a foam that conformed to the skier's foot for a really close fit. Foam was soon displaced by later interior adjustment systems that provided a custom fit that, unlike the foam, could be readjusted for size changes or an entirely different pair of feet in the same size range.

The continued development of the ski shop owed a lot to the professionalism of Robin Smith and Chic Carlucci who assisted customers in the autumn when people were getting set for the coming winter. By that time, Robin had become director of the ski school and Chic, assistant director. Both taught at Letchworth Central School where Chic later became assistant principal. Even after retiring as principal in 1994, he continued as ski school director until 2004. Robin was a member of the national demo team which established standards for American ski instructors. He was up to the minute on advances in all ski equipment and we came to rely heavily on his knowledge and expertise in selecting which brands and models to sell.

Also of great help in the ski shop over the years were high school students Joanne Livingston of Dalton, Rick Sanford of Nunda and Dena Spencer of Canaseraga I ran into Dena recently while visiting a friend in a nursing home and learned that she had gone on to earn a nursing degree.

Working at different times, this group along with regulars Delores Blakley, Barb Swain, daughter Jeanie (when she wasn't instructing) and me, often dealt with a three-deep row of customers assisting them to select gloves and supplying them with socks, underwear, and turtle neck shirts as requested. We always had a long counter of hats and racks of parkas and pants from which people could serve themselves, but space was too limited to provide self-service counters for all the other items we carried. We used the old lofts to store back-up supplies in their big shipping cartons. This involved a lot of running up and down stairs on busy days, mostly on my part, to replenish supplies in the smaller boxes on the shelves behind the counter.

Skis also underwent significant improvements. A single piece of shaped wood was replaced with a number of laminations that made possible lighter-weight, stronger and more maneuverable skis. The wood layer that formed the bottom of the ski was soon replaced with a slippery plastic (P-tex) that helped keep skis gliding smoothly even when the snow got sticky. The biggest development, however, was that instead of just being screwed-on sections of steel, edges became one long piece of steel incorporated into the structure of the ski.

Engineers designed ever more responsive skis to do the skier's bidding. The easy-to-turn models they designed for beginners contributed a lot to the growth of the sport by enabling beginners to learn faster. For racers and advanced recreational skiers they designed skis to hold course without wobbling at high speeds as well as skis for everybody in-between. Engineers are undoubtedly experimenting with new concepts of design even as they fine-tune and improve upon the latest concept of shorter, broader skis that have recently become popular.

An earlier trend to shorter skis, after going as far as it could, tended to moderate after overcoming the old fashioned idea that skis should be long enough to reach the wrist of an arm stretched overhead. Racers and advanced skiers rarely adopted the earlier shorter skis, or stopped short of extremes if they did, but many now use the more recent shorter but broader models.

It isn't only equipment that has undergone changes and improvements, however. Fashion designers soon saw an opportunity to expand their business and seized it. Their contribution of stretch pants which tapered down to a snug fit around the ankle to fit inside the ever higher new boot designs touched off a fashion revolution. Stretch pants were so flattering to all sizes and shapes that some women who had no intention of skiing bought an outfit in which they could frequent what was fast becoming the stylish atmosphere of base lodges. There was less World War II surplus army clothing to be seen on the slopes as skiers replaced it with lighter weight and better-insulated clothing with flattering lines in an array of fashionable colors.

It was amusing to see how manufacturers all seemed to change colors in harmony with each other from year to year and how an overall view of skiers on the slopes reflected these changes. e.g. One year red would predominate; the next year purple would become prominent. These color changes may have been instigated by fabric manufacturers as much as fashion designers, however. Whatever the reason, one year's flashes of bright orange would eventually be superseded by earthy tones. Skiing had become part of the fashion industry.

Fashion aside, thanks to developments in fabrics and insulation materials, today's ski wear manages to provide more warmth from head to toe than the bulky garments of years past.

Purchasing all this ever more sophisticated equipment for our shop meant that Dave and I had to attend the manufacturers' trade show every spring to keep abreast of all of the developments. Eunice Gaby made it possible for us to do so by looking after our children while we were away for almost a week. For the first decade or more, the shows were held in New York City in something called the Trade Show Building, which was located in the garment-manufacturing district where the streets were full of workers hustling racks of new styles from one place to another. The racks were usually covered - as much to conceal new ideas from competitors as to protect the garments from the weather.

It was still winter when we left Swain, but we drove into spring through blooming azaleas as we approached the city through New Jersey. It seemed like a big climate change for such a small change in latitude, but of course elevation was also a factor.

I remember every year passing several miles of Liberty cargo ships, left over from World War II, that were "mothballed" in the Hudson River. Thankfully, the need to reuse them never came. I don't know what became of these survivors of a conflict they had played a big part in winning. Some may have acquired new owners, but most have probably been reduced to scrap metal by now.

For the first five years or so, we stayed at the Paris Hotel, which we learned about from a small ad in The Saturday Review of Literature. A room and bath, albeit very small, cost just a little over $5 a night. Furthermore, the Paris had a swimming pool! What more could we ask? The first year we went, we reserved seats at three plays, but that was only for the first year. Our work in deciding what to buy with our ever-limited funds was so exhausting that I nodded off briefly during an excellent performance of My Fair Lady with Rex Harrison in the role of Professor Higgins.

We quickly learned that, far from a lark, trade show week would be one of our hardest working weeks of the year. There would be no time for the theatre, which was cheap then, and no time for the swimming pool, which was only open during the day when we were shopping for survival. Instead, our evenings were spent reviewing the material we had collected during the day. Our decisions would have been less critical if we had had more money to invest. As it was, mistakes could have been disastrous for our entire enterprise.[22]

---

[22] Jeanie: By the 1970s we had joined forces with Gary Muxworthy and Pittsford's Muxworthy's Ski Loft to qualify for quantity discounts. We had a warm, friendly relationship that lasted for decades, well past our tenure at Swain. Gary used to give us a pre-stuffed turkey every year for our Christmas dinner, and gave us a new television so we could watch the ski report, which he sponsored, in color.

When daughters Challice and Jeanie were in high school, we took them along with us to learn the trade. By that time the trade show had switched to rooms in the Statler Hilton so it was more efficient to stay there and avoid the subway commute. We missed the cosmopolitan atmosphere and friendliness of the Paris, however. Some people there were long-term residents who cooked in their rooms and we enjoyed the exotic aromas that seeped into the hall. One year, the dapper Japanese Olympic tumbling team was there at the same time we were.

There was a plaque painted with various flags alongside the desk in the small lobby. If you were unable to communicate with the cashier, you had only to point to your flag, and they would try to summon someone who could help. We were glad to see the same people working there every year and amazed that they, who saw so many different people in the course of a year, recognized us when we arrived.

Come to think of it, we must have stood out like sore thumbs because the same was true at the Paris Brest, a little French restaurant where we treated ourselves to one reasonably-priced gourmet meal a year. Everything in the small dining room was carried on under the watchful eye of Madame who looked as if she would pounce on any irregularities. The seating was at long narrow tables where you sat across from your partner and, at busy times, elbow to elbow with someone else. We usually had the same waitress or at least were able to speak to her. She had come over to earn money for her retirement before returning to France. I think it was one of the Rochester ski columnists, John Brown or Floyd King, who had recommended that we go there.

One year we went there only to find that it had disappeared. A passerby informed us that it had moved and directed us to the new location not far from the old one. The new restaurant was much larger and more up-to-date. We were glad for Madame and her employees' success but missed the old place with its postings of European soccer scores to keep customers up-to-date on how their favorite teams were doing.

One year we were informed that the trade show would be held in Las Vegas. Groan. Why did we have to go way out there? We soon found out that airline tickets were subsidized, lodging was cheaper, and the outdoor atmosphere a lot cleaner. Food was also much cheaper, the only catch being that you had to walk through what seemed like almost half a mile of slot machines to get to the dining area, an acceptable trade-off as far as we were concerned as we weren't about to donate any money to the slots.

These conditions may, or may not, be true today. Las Vegas was just getting into stride in our day. I understand its size has increased many times since then.

We looked forward to seeing our suppliers every year, especially the smaller specialty manufacturers like Earl Miller and Mitch Cubberly, who had designed and manufactured two of the earliest release bindings, and importers like Max Hurni from Switzerland, who had become friends. Robin Smith was in his element as many professional skier friends like Jim Marble, who became a Swain Ski School instructor, spent their summers as sales representatives for various companies.

I especially remember, but not the name of two brothers who were New York City clothing manufacturers. They didn't know anything about skiing but saw an opportunity to expand their business. At the first show we attended, they were offering a well-made nylon anorak at a very good price. We pointed out that it needed a hood. The next morning they summoned us in from the hall to show us their new samples complete with hoods. They told us they had gone to their factory the night before. With no employees on hand at night, they had taken their wives along to produce the new model. They must have sold well because the brothers became regular exhibitors at subsequent shows.

Despite being one of the toughest work weeks of the year, we always looked forward to renewing our relationship with folks like this just as we looked forward to seeing our own customers every autumn and winter.

Maude and Fred Blakley in their home.

Barb and Ted Swain at the ticket counter

"As it was in the beginning..." - The barn that became the base lodge.

Base lodge at the stage where the entire inside of the barn was utilized by skiers before any additions other than entryway at left were made. Windows in our abode in loft over cow barn are defined by white curtains. The chicken coup at right houses the original pit toilets.

The base ledge after three additiions to original barn. The building to the right with white trim around the windows is Gunny's "Honey Barn." The white gable over the "Honey Barn" belongs to the Yencer's house. The roof of Erma Babcock's, later Barb and Ted Swain's house, appears over the roof of the original barn. The light-colored building on the right, now leveled, housed the ski area's office and our home.

The base lodge complex and restaurant as it is today

Dave and Bina

Swain sign, late 1950s. Swain was an early innovator of snowmaking technology.

Dave in his army surplus anorak, which reversed to a white side for camouflage against snow. Poles may have been army surplus as well. Stretch pants and insulated parkas were still to come.

Andy, Jeanie, Challice and Janet display Swain's award for the most popular booth at a Buffalo ski show. The booth was amateurish compared to other, more expensive displays but managed to attract the most visitors with carnival-like games of skill.

Christmas card. We resorted to individual photos after failing to get an acceptable shot of all four. The |_| is the base of a green felt Christmas tree topped with foil star added by children which lent a touch of color to an otherwise black and white card.

Above: Nobody looks happy, no doubt due to the difficulty of getting everybody in place on a hot day for this photo which appeared in "The (Hornell) Evening Tribune." The occasion was for a report on the story hour Eunice conducted for local kids that summer. Back row: Lyle Weaver, Jeanine Swain, Eunice Gaby, Michael Wirt, Andy. Middle row: Challice, Michael Underwood, Bob Blakley, Rodney Swain, Jeanie, Dale France, Lisa Whitney. Front row: Mitchell May, Terry Klopf, Toni Klopf, Janet.

Above, Steve Baker, Kenny Buckland, Jeanie, Andy, and Buzzy (Phillip) Baker display cumulative season trophies from slalom ski races arranged and run by Kenny.

Right: the Swain Post Office

"Heavy" David Maul at the lift that now bears his name

Lyle Weaver, Harry Weaver and Bill Jenkins take a brief photo break

A happy group of spoiled mid-week skiers L to R: Bina, Dave, Dick Stopler of Geneseo, Dean Blades of Hornell, Bill and Lee White of Perry and Marge Edgerton of Rochester. Marge's husband Dick was probably the photographer.

Dean Blades greets a friend

Lee White wearing a Bousquet tow gripper

Demo Team Practice

Bina chats with Marge Edgerton.

Terry Johnson makes a repair in the ski shop

Killy, pronounced "Keely" after French Olympian Jean Claude Killy, hitches a ride down on Janet's back after demanding a ride up on the chairlift.

Dave and Bina at the top of Wheel's Run c. 1980

Daughter Jeanie and husband Jim Pownall, spring skiing c. 1982. The author wishes to express deep appreciation for the computer expertise J and J contributed to this book.

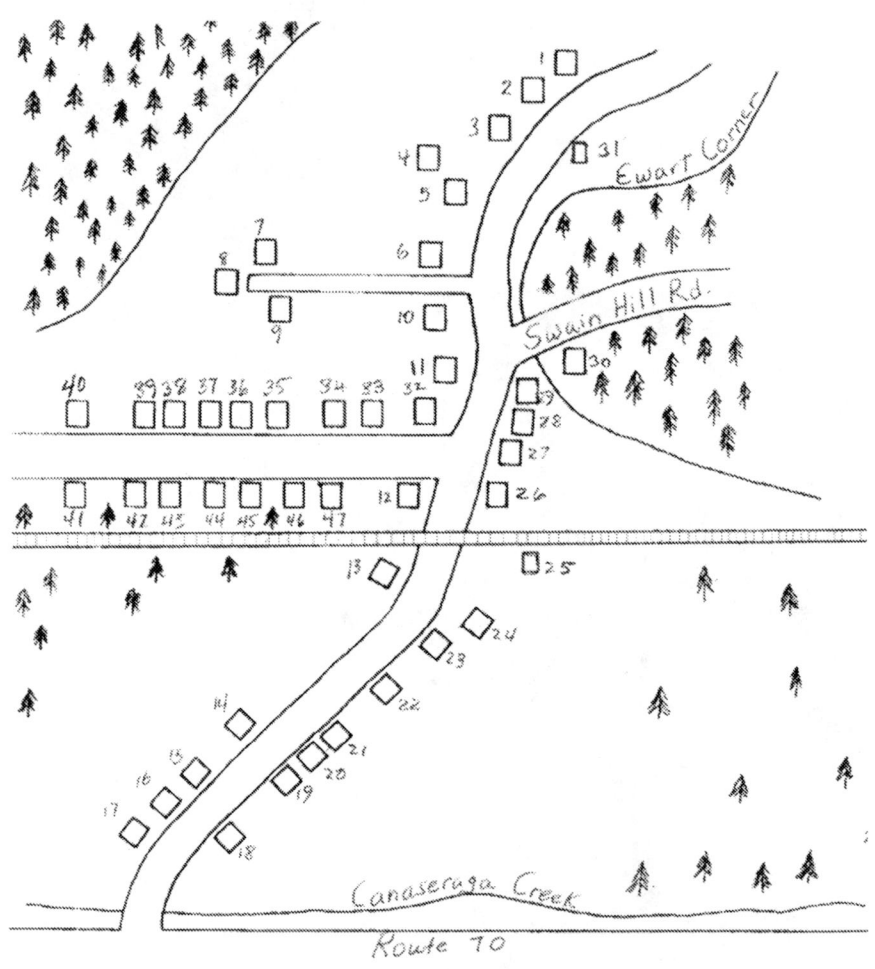

1940s Swain sketched by Matthew McLeod James

Swain Map Legend

1. Herthel & Alton Spencer. (Demolished)
2. Luella & Ernie Blakley. Now Downhill Drew's restaurant.
3. John Brewer plus Leon and Orsina (Underwood) Spike. (Demolished)
4. Erma Gleason Babcock's barn that became the base lodge.
5. Erma Gleason Babcock.
6. Agnes & Myrl ("Gunny") Yencer.
7. Margaret (Underwood) and Norman. (Demolished)
8. Mr & Mrs Livergood. (Demolished)
9. Emily ("Grandma") Dodge. (Demolished)
10. Anna & Ray Wirt.
11. Effie & Mel Cobin.
12. Maude & Fred Blakley, store.
13. Lula & Ben Blakley.
14. Barn - Marilyn Weidman (town historian) remembers this building as a barn.
15. Ruth & Glen Yencer.
16. Grace & Omar Boyd.
17. Elsie & Fred Neetz.
18. Clyde & Howard Macomber.
19. Clyde Macomber.
20. Ruth & Rev. Frank Karr (minister and mail carrier).
21. Jenny Pitcher.
22. Charlotte & Phil Hamilton.
23. Esther & John Harvey.
24. Joe Blakley, former town hall. (Demolished)
25. Grandma Blakley.
26. Helen & Ken Merriman, grocery store. Now Sierra Restaurant and Bar.
27. Methodist Church.
28. Gladys Newville.
29. Evangelical Church, now United Methodist Church.
30. Eleanor & Robert Shoemaker.
31. Joe and Leonard (Doc) Underwood. (Demolished)
32. Marie & Eldred (Dutch) Ludwig. Original post office.
33. Nora Mess. (Demolished)
34. Julia & Lawrence Weaver. (Demolished)
35. Anna & Delbert France. (Demolished)
36. Marion & Clare Macomber. (Demolished)
37. Ruth & Carl Sleight. (Demolished)
38. Rosamond & Sydney May. (Demolished)
39. Rosetta & Del Delaney. (Demolished)
40. Carl & Pearl Underwood.
41. Dolly & Rudy Underwood.
42. Lula & Leo Griffith.
43. Mary & Charles May.
44. Gertrude ("Gertie") Wood.
45. Lillian & Kenneth Carnes.
46. Eunice and Lester Gaby.
47. Dolores & Hugh Swain.

(See expanded legend in Appendix)

The author, front and center, at a University of Rochester ski trip to Old Forge, c. 1942.

Money

Money was always our biggest problem right from the start. It waxed and waned at the whim of the weather but never went away.

With our wartime savings of less than $3,000 depleted by our need for a car in order to search for a location, we were dependent on our two modest incomes that combined amounted to less than $5,000 - actually just $4,000 to start with. Keep in mind, however, that it was back in the 40's and everything cost less. Our biggest expense was rent at $40 a month which included heat and electricity. You could buy an unlimited Rochester city bus pass good for one week for $3. A bushel of apples or tomatoes could be bought for a dollar or less, and a pound of bananas or a can of soup was as little as a nickel. We weren't any worse off than most other young post-war couples, except that the ski area consumed most of our paychecks and kept demanding more than we actually had to give it.

Having both grown up during the Great Depression (the one that started with the stock market crash in 1929) turned out to be a valuable background for budding entrepreneurs in the 40's. My father, Thomas Cant Aitchison often discussed the family finances with me when

I accompanied him on the long walks he liked to take. He and my mother had bought the family's first car, a new blue Dodge, just before the crash and had to give it up when his pay as an electrical engineer working for the General Electric Company was suddenly cut in half. My parents, who were British immigrants, were in the process of buying their first house and wisely gave priority to meeting mortgage rather than car payments. Dad used to log over five miles a day on foot getting to and from work

My mother, nee Winifred Maude Binless (hence Bina), was a good manager and took pride in wasting nothing. My sister Elizabeth and I still have a good laugh now and then about the hard little bullets of leftover peas that often turned up alone or in leftover fried potatoes. That is not a fair example of the output of a cook renowned for her Yorkshire pudding. It is, however, a good example of how she avoided wasting anything. (I have just recently discovered that I rather like the flavor of canned peas after having disdained them for years.)

My elementary school had a book called *The Five Little Peppers and How they Grew,* "Pepper" being the last name of a family whose members led a good life in spite of being in poor financial circumstances. The one thing that sticks in my mind about the story is that Mrs. Pepper saved her basting thread so that she could use it again for her next sewing job. That, and other Horatio Alger-type stories of thrift-conquering-poverty made an obviously lasting impression on a child growing up during the big depression which dragged on through much of the 1930's.

I had an allowance of 50 cents a week, disproportionately generous for those times, but there was not much left for discretionary spending by the time I had perhaps bought a bottle of ink for school (no ball point pens then), paid out weekly dues to scouts, various school clubs and the church offering plate. Still, by saving the nickel or dime that was sometimes left over, I was able to buy a Pocket Book now and then. The first one I bought was Thornton Wilder's *The Bridge of San Luis Rey*. They cost 25 cents in those days. Movies were just 10 cents for kids. Bus fare was only six cents, but I always walked the mile uptown to the movies and to school as did all my friends and even my mother - in the moderately high (Cuban) heels that were her normal everyday wear.

Dave must have had equally frugal habits because his mother discovered a bank book showing a balance of almost $200 while cleaning his room when he was in the Marine Corps. We uncharacteristically blew most of it on dining and dancing after he was discharged from the marines and waiting to be called up again. This was during my senior year in college. I was working at Strong Memorial Hospital for six hours a day seven days a week and should have been studying in the time that remained, but being with Dave seemed more important. I was enrolled in an independent study program and managed to get the two required weekly papers researched and written by getting by on very little sleep.

Reverting to our usual abstemious habits after the war, we managed to get Swain up and running by not spending any money on anything we didn't actually have to have. It wasn't as hard as it sounds because we worked on the area every day that we were not required to be at our jobs. We didn't at first own a house that needed maintenance and improvements. We inherited, or had the opportunity to buy cheaply, enough used furniture to move into an unfurnished flat and later a tenant farm house in Henrietta. We were the grateful recipients of all sorts of items being replaced by our parents and Dave's Rochester relatives.

My father once remarked that he never knew anybody who could stuff as much stuff into an ordinary car as we could. Sometimes we had to tie large items on the roof, but we always managed somehow. Unlike most newlyweds, we didn't have time to worry whether things matched. The fact that they had belonged to relatives or friends of relatives just made these hand-me-downs seem comfortable - like old friends.

I have written elsewhere about how Fred Blakley, Gail Combs and Harry Knights extended us credit. Dave wrote in his account of the starring role of the Bank of Castile, which was willing to issue loans, modest by today's standards, when we needed to buy something for the area we couldn't pay for until after the next ski season. Bud (Charles) VanArsdale at the bank might have been influenced by the fact he liked to ski. Fred probably thought a ski area would be good for the town, but he and Harry, both successful business men, probably got vicarious satisfaction from helping a hard-working young couple to make a start.

Our parents, each set having raised two children were comfortably off, but neither pair was anywhere close to being what you might call well-to-do. We didn't expect or seek any help from them but were glad to accept the stipend my parents offered so I could stay home after Challice was born during a particularly bleak financial period. We also accepted at another time of severe financial crisis when Dave's parents, Alice Mae (Challice) and Ray McLeod Robinson, offered to share with us the proceeds from the sale of Aunt Nell's cottage, which she had left to them sort of in trust for Dave. She had always intended to leave him the cottage but had sold it instead when she saw we wouldn't have time to use it and would have been saddled with upkeep and taxes.

Along the way, there were hundreds of minor financial crises like the time I ordered from the Henrietta postmaster a box of stamped envelopes with the area's return address printed on them. Unfortunately, we didn't have the money, the princely sum of $15, first class postage being just three cents at the time, to pay for them when they arrived. I knew we could come up with it in a couple of weeks or so, but the postmaster had no guarantee of that and no doubt feared she would be stuck with 500 stamped envelopes with our address on them. The fact that it sticks in my mind is an indication of how stressful the situation became.

That event was trivial compared to hundreds of others, the biggest of which was being unable to pay most of our employees more than minimum wage. Whenever we did occasionally manage to get a little ahead, the legal minimum would be raised soon afterwards putting us back on square one. I particularly remember this because of Dave's telling me that Lula Griffith, who ably managed a food counter in the Shawmut Room, had, with tears in her eyes, expressed her appreciation for a small raise, saying that she had never before been paid more than the minimum wage for her work. She must have been in her 50's or even 60's by then and was a very conscientious worker who gave at least 150% of the effort that could normally be expected from anyone.

The worst came after a very poor season when we were saddled with more than the usual amount of debt and couldn't take on any more. Dave had to tell Gunny Yencer we could no longer pay him. Gunny, then our only full-time employee, had done a really good job as slope manager for several years and did not deserve to be laid off, but the alternative would have been to work for nothing in hope of being repaid later. It was one of our worst times and hurtful for all concerned.

Most of our employees deserved more, but the money just wasn't there. It was years before we were able to take a very modest salary for ourselves. We had been living off the money we got from selling our house. We qualified for the government's surplus food program but didn't have time to drive to Belmont to get it. We did get a trickle down benefit, however, because our neighbors, Orsina and Leon Spike, had no use for the rolled wheat and passed it on to us. Other recipients scornfully referred to the rolled wheat as "chicken feed" because that's where most of it wound up. Fortunately for us, the Spikes had no chickens. It produced some of the best cookies I ever made and many a hearty bowl of cereal. It wasn't, and still isn't, available in ordinary grocery stores, but I recently saw some in a health food store at a rather fancy price.

In winter, there were usually leftovers from the cafeteria that could be scrambled into something. At the end of the season in March or April, there would be a bonanza of leftovers that could be frozen for later use. The only problem was lack of freezer space. Sometimes the season would end with an unexpected thaw leaving us with space-consuming hot dog and hamburger rolls. Waste not want not. Sliced thin and dipped in egg batter, they became French toast and the equivalent in our children's minds of my mother's fried peas in mine. Knowing what I know today, I would have tried to avoid feeding my family white bread, but didn't hesitate to take advantage of any available free food in those days.

When it was time to shop for school clothes, we went to a used clothing store in Arkport, but were careful to buy good new shoes as often as needed. It was harder then when sneakers were not the norm. We usually wound up with Hush Puppies, much to youngest daughter Janet's disgust. We didn't scrimp on ski equipment either, even buying the children buckle boots when most adults were still wearing and buying new laced boots. This was less extravagant than it sounds because the children were able to put them on themselves at times when it would have been difficult for us to take the time to do so. For several years, until Andy's size surged, we were able to hand them down from one to the other. Challice, being the oldest was always the recipient of new boots, but the others had the advantage of not having to break them in.

It was really neglectful that our children had to learn on their own. Because of our work load, giving them good equipment was the best we could do for them. We didn't know that Challice, the oldest, was riding the rope tows until we found the telltale holes in her knitted mittens and provided her with proper tow mitts. Like all their local contemporaries, they all became excellent skiers just by doing it even on the less responsive equipment of those days.

But to get back to wider area financial problems, which are strangely less clear in my mind than scores of little ones, probably because the big ones were mostly handled by Dave in collaboration with Bud VanArsdale at the Bank of Castile. Our first really big loan was extended by the Small Business Administration (SBA). It seems it must have been to finance the area's first chair lift. We learned that such a loan might be available at ski area operators' conference while having breakfast with Joe Tso. (It's funny how some names pop up while others, which I have even better reason to remember remain buried.) Joe told us about the loan he had received for his area in the eastern part of the state. Our application was accepted. I have an idea that we were a year late with the last repayment installment, but, unlike many SBA loan recipients, we did pay up in full.

Before that, we had financed the first T-bar by selling stock in the area. The sale fell short of the amount we needed, but it was enough to permit the project to go ahead. We actually even paid a dividend after the first year, but it was an expense the area couldn't really afford, and we probably had to borrow money to meet expenses before the beginning of the next season. There were no dividends after that. I remember only one stockholder complaining at the annual meeting, and he was overridden by others. The majority of the stockholders told us they were satisfied with free skiing as a return on their investment. I think it cost $1,000 for a Lifetime individual pass and $2,000 for a family so it was really a pretty good deal for people like us with four kids.

We were never free from money worries, however. It was harder on Dave than me because he was dealing with the big picture while I was dealing more directly with details over which I had more control. Everything always depended on the weather over which we had no control before snowmaking came along to reduce, but by no means entirely overcome, our dependence on natural meteorological events.

In addition to the weather, another factor over which we had no control was competition. When we first opened, skiers came to us from Buffalo, Ohio and Canada as well as Rochester. We weren't the only skiers who dreamed of developing a ski area in western New York, however. Other areas sprang up south of Buffalo intercepting most of our Buffalo, Ohio and Canadian customers, who naturally chose to ski closer to home.

Fortunately, the number of people skiing kept growing so there were enough to go around even after the advent of snowmaking made it feasible for areas to open and operate closer to Rochester.

Somehow, aided greatly by the development of snowmaking, we managed to survive the poor snow winters so that the area was in sound financial shape when Dave, influenced by the premature deaths of several of our contemporaries who ran ski areas, felt a strong urge to retire. Our children were not old enough to take over. The logical person to do so was the head of the ski school, Robin Smith who had contributed so much to the area's success by organizing, selling and running special programs for area schools. So that Robin could continue improving the area by replacing the three remaining T-bars with chairlifts, we were glad to forego for the time being the small share of the proceeds that had been agreed upon. We felt we had made a good decision until the seemingly prosperous area suddenly went bankrupt and we were essentially left with our social security checks, which were based on the very modest salaries we had been able to pay ourselves.

SKI AREA'S EFFECT ON THE HAMLET OF SWAIN

Named for one of its earliest settlers, Samuel Swain, who, like me, had migrated from western Massachusetts,[23] the little hamlet lies nestled in the hills about four miles west of Canaseraga.[24] Swain was once a bustling community at the junction of two creeks, Canaseraga and Ewart, and three railroads, the Erie and the Pittsburgh, Shawmut & Northern (PS&N) and the Allegany Central (which was eventually acquired by the Pennsylvania Railroad).

---

[23] A least I had always thought this to be the case from information on a deed until Dolores (Mrs. Hugh) Swain loaned me a carefully-transcribed copy of Samuel's detailed day-by-day oral account of the family's westward journey which clearly states that the family headed west from Vermont. Dolores thinks it not unlikely that their residence had previously been in Tyringham, Massachusetts as I recalled, however.

[24] I haven't heard anyone say CanaserAHga for a long time. When we arrived back in the 1940's pronunciation seemed to be more or less equally divided between AYga and the traditional AHga pronunciation for Indian names ending aga. Daughter Challice recalls it was the old-timers who said AHga, but it "kind of migrated" to AYga during the last half century. Taking a cue from Canaseraga Central School principal Dayton Murray, I used to say AHga, but have drifted to AYga in keeping up with the times.

Today, only the Erie, now called the Norfolk and Southern, remains in operation after undergoing three name changes. In 1960 it merged with the Lackawanna to become the Erie Lackawanna until 1976 when it became Conrail under a government reorganization program to rescue financially strapped railroads. It wasn't until 1999 that it became the Norfolk and Southern, but I still think of it "the Erie." The Erie played a much bigger role in local people's lives, after all, and, as far as I know, there's no song about the Norfolk and Southern.

Starting with "In 14 hundred and 92, Columbus sailed the ocean blue," a series of stanzas depicting historical events is divided by the chorus

"Erie, Erie, I Ree O
    Erie, Erie, I Ree O
        Erie, Erie, I Ree O
            Workin' on the railroad."

The Allegany Central Railroad appears on one of daughter Challice's deeds dated 1897. Its tracks lay just west of those of the Erie. It ran from Friendship to Swain (or Swains as the railroads were more likely to call it) via Angelica, which was then the county seat. Its purpose was to connect the growing network of railroads in the northern part of the county with the growing network in the south. Also known at one time as the Allegany Central & Western, parts of it were taken over by the PS&N and eventually the Pennsylvania as ownership was shuffled around. A report in the Allegany County Republican of December 6, 1882, a year of frenzied railroad construction in the area, noted that "the whistle of the locomotive is heard by the most remote inhabitant [of Allegany County]." This must have been especially true in Swain.

The PS&N, better known locally simply as "the Shawmut," is no more. It was torn up shortly before we settled on Swain as the location for our ski area-to-be. Only faint traces of the old rail bed are discernable on the east side of the main valley carved out by Canaseraga Creek, most of it having been obliterated by improvements to what is now Route 70. The rail bed, gradually rising to the south along the west side of the valley, is pretty much intact, however, and comprises part of the Finger Lakes Trail (FLT) serving hikers and cross-country skiers. The east-west FLT stretches across most of New York State connecting the north-south Appalachian Trail with the Bruce Trail in Canada.

Despite its cinder surface being buried under well over half a century's accumulation of leaves that supports a growing population of trees and other plants, the rail bed along the west side of the valley is easily identifiable mainly because it was graded across the nearly vertical hillside. The year-round spring that furnished water for the engines to produce steam continues to flow. Here and there lie the deteriorating remains of an old chestnut railroad tie or two. Most of the ties were salvaged along with the rails when the Shawmut was ripped up in 1947, the same year we began working on the ski area.

The raised horseshoe bend that enabled trains to cross the valley high and dry above Canaseraga Creek and chug backward as far as what is now the bottom of Mile Sweep Trail is still prominent, but it is no longer possible to pick out the exact location of the depot. Mark Heath, Erma Gleason Babcock's father, was in charge of the depot, which was also a Wells Fargo station. We found an old Wells Fargo sign painted on metal in the basement of Erma's barn. Despite our strong intention to preserve it, it somehow disappeared.

Extending the Shawmut from Canaseraga to Swain involved laying about an extra seven miles of track. This was done primarily to gain elevation before heading south over the hills to Angelica, but also because Swain was a place of significant commerce around the time the 1800's became the 1900's.

With automobile ownership mostly in the future, the railroads were the major source of transportation as late as the early 1900's. Students from Swain and the surrounding area wanting to attend high school rode the Shawmut back and forth to Angelica. Agnes Yencer and Eunice Gaby were among those who did so. As depicted in The Music Man, salesmen used to take the train to call on their customers along the line. Ordinary people would take the train to visit friends and relatives to avoid spending most of the day getting back and forth via horse and wagon.

In places, the section of rail bed, that is part of the FLT, is partially obstructed by large blocks of shale that frost has pried loose from exposed bedrock above the old roadbed. Smaller chunks of rock regularly tumble from the cliff along this section as water and frost continue to enter and expand fissures in the rock.

An elevated section known as "Fifty Fill," built up to carry the trains across Fox Gully, is still there except that it was breached when Fred Blakley's crew attempted to recover the giant "tubes" (culverts) that allowed the stream to flow underneath. This was done to supply scrap metal for the war effort during World War II. The crew succeeded in extricating the tubes all right but not in dragging them to a road or railroad. Possibly, they were abandoned where they still lie because the war was coming to a close or possibly, judging from their present appearance, because the metal was deemed unworthy of salvaging.

Swain even had a hotel. Unfortunately, like all the other buildings in town, it was built of wood and burned down just a few years before it might have been returned to use for skiers. After years of producing good vegetables at the hands of Dutch Ludwig, its position on the corner of Main and Mill now serves as a parking lot for the Mountainside Inn, a lodging complex formed by adding to Effie and Mel Cobin's house on Main Street.

In addition to Main and Mill streets, "the lane" once had three houses, the Riley Ulster house at the base of the hill that served as the ski patrol building for a couple of decades, the parsonage, and our home and ski area office purchased from Margaret (Underwood) and Norman Didas. None of these houses remains today. Gone too is the magnificent balm of Gilead (a.k.a poplar) tree outside our house that rose over all the other trees and man-made structures on the floor of the hamlet.

In the 1800's, there were three sawmills along what is now Mill Street as well as what is referred to as "the largest wooden bucket factory in the world." I can't vouch for the validity of this claim, but there was certainly a wooden bucket factory and also a broom factory. The latter became the home of Dolores and Hugh Swain and their children Ronald, Gary, Jeanine, Rodney, and Gregory.

Irene Szabo, president of the Finger Lakes Trail Conference, to whom I am indebted for much of this historical information, informs me that the sawmills burned wood to produce steam to power saws to saw up yet more wood. This was because Canaseraga Creek did not fall fast enough year round along this stretch to generate sufficient power, and its faster-flowing tributaries did not consistently carry enough water to do so. This condition changes just on the other side of Canaseraga where a waterfall powered "the old mills," and a power company built a small dam to generate electricity.

Next to the west side of the Erie tracks where they crossed Main Street, two stores, fronting good-sized houses faced each other across the road. The one on the north side of the street was still a functioning grocery store when Dave and I first arrived. It was operated by Helen and Ken Merriman followed by Hilda and Harold Kerr. After the Kerrs moved away, it was taken over by a couple named Dietz followed by Bill Whitney who was numerous times elected to serve as Town of Grove Superintendent. Bill operated it as sort of a forerunner of a fast food outlet serving primarily hamburgers and hot dogs. With the exception of skiing weekends, there just weren't enough people in the area to support it, and Bill had a working dairy farm to take care of in addition to the all the town's roads.

As people became more mobile, small country stores, including this one, succumbed to the lower prices and greater variety offered by supermarkets and cooperative stores in surrounding villages and cities. These country stores were a vital part of rural communities before the automobile replaced the horse and wagon. Swain once even had two of them. Mutually beneficial bartering for eggs, butter and garden produce was customary. The Swain store was not closed for long, however. George Redfield came to town from somewhere out west and turned it into a year- round bar and restaurant he called "The Sierra," now owned and operated by Teresa and Jim Crawford.[25]

The ski area has a more posh second-storey restaurant always open in winter, intermittently open in summer but usually available for special

---

[25] Until the summer of 2007, the only other year-round eatery in town in Luella and Ernie Blakley's old house at the bottom of Brewer Slope belonged to our son, Andy. Known as Downhill Drew's, it caters primarily to skiers, but was until 2007 open a couple of nights a week year-round. His twin sons David and Colin enjoy working there.

events including proms for area schools. In 2007, however, as part of a program to establish year-round resort status, it is open Friday through Sunday.

By the time we got there, the store across from what is now The Sierra served primarily as an office for Fred Blakley and his lumber operations conducted from behind a huge roll-top desk. Fred's wife, Maude, ruled over their residence in the house behind, but Fred was king and the unofficial mayor of Swain in the store front.[26] Son Andy now conducts his business from Fred's desk which he bought from Junior. More significantly, our oldest daughter Challice bought the whole building from Junior. She calls it "Maude's Country Store" in honor of Maude, operates a pizza and sub shop in the store front during the ski season and practices massage therapy in a room set aside for the purpose in the residential part of the building.

Fred sold gas from a pump out front and used to sell motor oil and other items he stocked for his own business inside. There is still a hole in the storefront floor through which rope could be pulled up from a large reel in the basement and cut off in lengths to suit customer requirements.

Mel Cobin also sold gas from a pump in front of his and Effie's house a hundred or so feet farther up the road. I'm told they also had sort of a general store in a front room at one time. These two rather casual enterprises, in addition to the grocery store and the post office comprised the business district of the hamlet. Ski school instructors who hailed

---

[26] Daughter Jeanie who used to spend time with Maude recalls that Fred used to nap at his desk with hands folded over his stomach and his partially-amputated middle finger sticking straight up.

from larger communities later satirically referred to this small area at the intersection of Main and Mill Streets as "downtown Swain."

The United States Post Office was just around the corner on Mill Street. It consisted of a small room with its own entrance in Marie and Eldred ("Dutch") Ludwig's house where they lived with their children Kit, Helen, Lois, Neal and Esther. Esther and husband John Dieter with children Karen and Michael (Mike) moved there after Marie and Dutch passed on. Mike, wife Debby and children Aaron, Angela and Amy have occupied this home since Esther and John died.

When we first arrived, the mail was delivered and picked up twice a day by passing trains. I remember this because Eunice Gaby received a pittance (I think it was $200 a year, less than a dollar a day) for placing the outgoing mailbag on a special hook where the trains could snag it as they passed. The incoming mailbag was thrown on the ground, with varying accuracy, for her to find and pick up. The job required standing by the tracks in all kinds of weather to make certain it was not interfered with either after arrival or before departure. I can remember seeing Eunice waiting there before I knew her or realized what she was doing. Sometimes her youngest child, Keith, would be at her side, sheltering against her from the wind that races like an express train along the tracks in that location.

The post office retained its room in the Ludwig home even after Marie retired and Lillian Carnes succeeded her as postmaster. In 1973, Lillian had a special building constructed on a corner of the land on the other side of the railroad tracks where she and Kenneth had situated their new prefabricated home. While probably not the smallest, it has the distinction of being one of the smallest post offices still operating in the country. Because of the volume of mail it handles, partly due to the ski area, it has escaped the widespread elimination of small post offices that has taken place in recent years.

The 42 or so antique mail boxes with combination locks were transferred to the new building and remained in use until 2004 when they were replaced with 150 new boxes to accommodate the growing number of new homes in the area. We are told that old boxes are now in a Washington museum.

I never saw anyone use the combination locks on the old boxes because Marie or Lillian always handed us our mail. Dave and I never even knew what the combination to our box was. Instead of being equipped with combination locks, the new boxes require the use of a key which we are expected to use and for which we were charged $1.00. It isn't always easy to empty a full box over the speed bump-like ridge on the bottom and past the projecting metal on the sides, particularly when there are several magazines and catalogues. Whoever is on duty is always willing to help, however.

What is really hard is that boxes in the top rows are above eye-level for almost everybody but professional basketball players, and the bottom row is below knee-level, exactly 12 inches above the floor to be exact, about right for a cat. Thankfully, our old Box 26 turned out to about hip high so I neither have to grope over my head nor kneel down on the floor to see into the box. I feel for those who wound up with a location that is awkward for them.

After Lillian retired as postmaster, we had several temporary officers-in-charge, but now have Julie Leaty in that position. Lillian's daughter

Joan still works there Saturday mornings and when the postmaster is temporarily needed elsewhere. Outgoing mail is still postmarked with a rubber stamp but there is now a computer behind the counter. Mail is delivered and picked up once a day rather than twice as of old, and a first class stamp costs 41 instead of 3 cents. The annual box fee is now $40, up from $8 in 1996. Otherwise, the service is much the same, i.e. personal and friendly, and people still linger to chat when it isn't busy.

Lillian retired as postmaster after she turned 79 (seventy-nine!) in 1992, but continued to live next door in the prefabricated home she and husband Ken bought after selling their home on Mill Street, where they had raised daughters Barbara, Sandra, Joan, Dianne and Nancy. Just recently, however, her 97 (ninety-seven) years made it prudent to move to an assisted living facility in Hornell where, relieved of building maintenance and cooking and housekeeping chores, she continues to keep busy reading books and doing crossword puzzles.

After Lillian retired, her daughter Joan (pronounced Jo-ann) Carpenter served as officer-in-charge for a number of years and, since officially retiring, has substituted for a series of temporary officers-in-charge and present postmaster, Julie Leaty. Joan lives in a new house built with her late husband Greg on land they reserved after selling to a group of skiers the home where they had lived with sons, David, Craig and Sheldon, in what had been Lula and Ben Blakley's imposing house. Greg worked at Lucidol but took up skiing with sufficient skill and enthusiasm to become a ski school instructor in spite of the fact that he had lost part of one hand in a tractor accident.

Industry was represented in our time by the sawmill, now dismantled, located next to Ewart Creek in the area behind the grocery store.

Farming was, and still is, but to a lesser extent these days, carried on atop the surrounding hills and along the valley carved out by Canaseraga Creek where Route 70 leads to Dalton and points west as well as north and south. Former farm fields are sprouting homes along the roads.

Gunny Yencer, who worked at Foster Wheeler in Dansville, also had a small business producing honey. The bees gathered the honey, of course, but Gunny provided them with hives and had an extractor that separated the honey from the wax. There was a lot of buzzing, not all of it from the bees, in and around his "Honey Barn" every autumn.

Ewart Creek used to meander at will through town until folks got fed up with the occasional flooding and confined it to a channel on the north side of Main Street. The channel was reinforced with sections of the metal hulls from scrapped ships. Some of these rusted steel sheets are still visible farther up stream and at the base of the more conspicuous modern steel retaining wall, which in one place rises about three feet higher than the old one. The creek has to be cleaned out every few years as storms cause this channel to fill up with rocks washed down from farther upstream.

I can remember water sneaking over the old steel barrier a few times but not seriously until June of 1972 when slow-moving Hurricane Agnes seemed to stall over the area and let loose most of the water she had picked up over the Atlantic on Pennsylvania and New York. Before Hurricane Hugo hit seven years later, Agnes had caused the most damage of any hurricane on record. During the storm, Ewart Creek reverted to its old habits and cut across yards and the ski area parking lots on its way to Canaseraga Creek. At least one small fish was stranded at the bottom near the Clark lift house.

During this deluge, Dave and I worked to clear an old channel around the base of the area in order to keep the water away from the houses along Mill Street. At one point I was swept off my feet when the current caught the full length raincoat I was wearing because more practical garments were still wet from previous use. The following summer Chuck May bulldozed the narrow channel to a wider depression, which as far as I know has done the job ever since.

Acting upon a complaint that water running down the ski slopes was flooding basements, I followed one streamlet uphill on foot to the very top where water from falling rain stood two inches deep everywhere. As water does the world over, it ran downhill. Reverting to a favorite childhood activity of building snow dams in the cobblestone gutters of the hilly street where I grew up, I began to move sticks and stones and fallen logs to divert the water across the top of the hill. It wasn't long before I had created a sizeable stream headed away from the slopes toward Fox Gully which would carry the water into Canaseraga Creek below town.[27] It was only a minor diversion in what had become a watery world, but I took a great deal of satisfaction from it even though I realized it was of minimal practical value.

Less satisfying was the necessary chore of emptying the rain barrels in the lofts inside the base lodge. The roof over the old barn had started to leak a little, but not much, along the north side. In order to postpone the expense of redoing the roof, Dave had ingeniously installed indoor

---

[27] Daughter Jeanie recalls working with me and, 27 years later, using the techniques learned from the experience to divert water from her home in Pennsylvania during Hurricane Floyd. She also facilitates the drainage on her suburban road whenever there is a deluge, which is not infrequent. She was surprised to receive a complaint from a man (who thought she was employed by the town) that she'd better hurry up and get the drainage grid clear before the water backed up into his driveway.

eaves troughs directing the water into big garbage cans that only had to be bailed out occasionally - until hurricane Agnes hit and made it necessary to empty them every couple of hours. We took turns responding to the alarm clock and carrying the water outside in pails to add to the shallow lake that covered the ground everywhere.

More seriously, I am reminded that Canaseraga Creek was flowing across Main Street cutting the hamlet off from the state road. Worse yet, it was lapping around the home of Elsie and Fred Neetz. Neighbors assembled in the rain with tractors and trucks to evacuate Elsie and Fred and their belongings before the water got any deeper, but Fred refused to budge, telling his would be rescuers that the house had withstood flooding in the past and would do so again this time. Fortunately, he turned out to be right.

Putting vivid memories of hurricane Agnes aside and getting back to what Swain was like in normal times after Dave and I first arrived, the hamlet had a well-built one-room school house with a floor several feet above the flood plane. It was under the jurisdiction of the Canaseraga Central School Board chaired at that time by Ross Kingston. The board had been wanting to close the school for some time because it was impractical to hire a teacher for so few children. The year before it was closed, they had paid Swain resident Gladys Newville to teach just two students, Linda Yencer and Jimmy Blowers.

There was some bitterness over the fact that in exchange for votes in support of building a central school in Canaseraga, the school board had promised to maintain an elementary school in Swain through third grade. Closing the school meant the school district was divested of what it considered a liability because it required hiring a teacher in addition to maintaining the building, which had no running water and a pit toilet. The town of Grove (including the hamlet of Swain) gained an undeniable asset in the form of a well-constructed building for community affairs, but at the cost of losing its own school. The fact that the building had no running water was easily remedied by carrying in a jug or two of drinking water at a time.

Ironically, voting is now conducted at the town highway shed farther up the road in deference to a law requiring voting places to have toilets. If it had remained a school, it seems likely the state would have required the school board to update the seldom-used privy tacked on to the back of the building. Among other improvements, this would have required drilling a well and installing a septic system.

This building, now the town hall for the Town of Grove, is surrounded by ski area parking lot. There was some bitterness in losing the local school, but the deal was sweetened by the building being sold for a dollar to the Town of Grove. After the school was closed, we bought all but the small plot surrounding the new town hall. By the time we moved there to operate the area full time, any young children reaching kindergarten age (including our own four as they turned five) joined the older ones on the school bus that took them to the central school in Canaseraga.

Today, the building is used almost exclusively for town board meetings, but has a history of being a polling place, a center for social events and even a youth recreation center when church minister John Hausman and wife Betsy occupied the parsonage. (Betsy later remodeled a small house on Main Street into an attractive modern residence.)

As I write, a proposal from the present ski area management to move the building farther up the road and update facilities so that voting can again take place there is under consideration. The ski area would benefit by gaining an unbroken parking lot with space to park a few more cars but this is outside the time frame I'm writing about. This book is more about the past than the present and certainly not about what might or might not happen in the future.

Swain also had two churches, one Methodist, the other Evangelical United Brethren, just a couple of doors from each other on the north side of Main Street. The Methodist church was closed a few years after we started the ski area for some reason, probably for lack of money because there were too few surviving members. I can remember Maude Blakley sputtering some years later about how the Evangelicals, who were probably given whatever interior furnishings they could use, had "marched right down and helped themselves" to extra chairs that she had personally loaned or donated to the church.

The Evangelical Church, now of United Methodist affiliation, is still going strong and welcomes skiers to Sunday services. The former parsonage on "the lane" was closed and belonged to Ski School Director, Chic Carlucci, and his wife Joan, also a certified instructor, until it was demolished to make more room for snow-grooming vehicles and the growing number of skiers. Chic and Joan bought Mary and Chuck May's old house on Mill Street where Chuck and Mary had lived with children, Steven, Mitchell, and twins Michelle and Brian. Mary and Chuck now live in the new house they built above Route 70 between Swain and Canaseraga, and the Carluccis have retired to a condo at a western ski area. Chic continued to run the ski school for a decade or so after he had retired as principal of Letchworth Central School in Castile.

The Methodist Church was converted to a house by Gunny Yencer for his newly married daughter Marilyn and husband Lynn Weidman. It has continuously afforded a home rented to several families over the years as people have come and gone.

So, was the ski area good for this small community or not? It certainly brought recognition to what had become a rather insignificant place as far as the world at large was concerned. It was a source of satisfaction for some that the hamlet of Swain became better known than the much larger communities of Canaseraga and Dalton which had village status. There were drawbacks, however. For one thing, the hamlet lay for the most part on the opposite (west) side of the valley from the main road (now Route 70) which tended to hug the bottom of the almost vertical side of Rattlesnake Hill. The hamlet's position off the beaten track spared residents from through traffic between Canaseraga and Dalton and Nunda. The only through traffic was to farms farther up Ewart Creek and on the hills above. There is more traffic today because there are more homes up the valley and beyond, but this is nothing in comparison to the influx of cars that occurs on weekends when the area is open for skiing.

After the railroads folded, or stopped carrying passengers, the once busy community of Swain became a sort of backwater out of the main stream. I'm guessing that even as late as the 1940's a third of the houses were still using outdoor privies as opposed to inside bathrooms. This was probably primarily due to lack of funds but perhaps also to a certain amount of reluctance to change. Contact with the outside world was available to anyone with a car, but people seemed contented without it - except to get to jobs in Hornell and Dansville, and wherever the section crew was working on the railroad. School buses took the children to school in Canaseraga. Television, which made a big difference, was still to come. Today, some folks commute as far as Corning, Rochester and Buffalo.

Swain was a wonderful place for families with children, and there were a lot of children in the 40' and 50's. Everybody knew everybody else, and there were many family ties binding people together. The generations intermingled more than we had ever experienced before. Small children were on a first-name basis with adults of all ages, a custom we quickly fell in with even though we had been brought up to use "Miss," "Mr.," and "Mrs." even for close family friends of our parents' generation. This informality did not that I know of apply to teachers, ministers or doctors, however, although son Andy, who was about five at the time, was once overheard yelling "Come on, Hausie Baby" to encourage preacher John Hausman to get a hit during an informal softball game. There were even odd occasions on which our pre-school children called me Bina instead of Mom.

Sometimes, but rarely, when there was a disagreement about something, the closeness could become a bit oppressive. I can remember once experiencing a feeling of relief as my view of the sky expanded as I climbed the steeper side of the valley to visit the Whitney sisters, Mary, Helen, Judy and Nellie in their farmhouse from which Judy ran a turkey farm. The road is so steep that it was closed in winter even during the many years when their brother Bill was serving as town highway superintendent. (They also had another brother, Harold who moved away after living with his family on Route 70 for a few years.) Everybody had to take a longer way around in winter, and I can remember having difficulty climbing even that road on more than one occasion before 4-wheel drive transmissions became available on passenger vehicles.

The demand for more housing attracted another entrepreneur, builder Jerry Livingston who built two attractive cabins alongside Canaseraga Creek, which were soon bought by skiers. Riding on that success, his brother Ron built two more and went on with two partners to build 16 townhouse condominiums. The condos are mostly owned by skiers and rented in summer to folks escaping from Florida's torrid summer weather. Most, if not all of the summer tenants had once lived in the area before they retired and moved to Florida. Because many still have family and friends in the area, returning for the summer is a bit like coming home. They are a community within the Swain community with unique customs like the Christmas and New Year parties held during the summer. Marilyn Weidman handles the business transactions and helps facilitate activities.

The lower hillside pastures of the Whitney farm overlooking the ski slopes now support a Swiss-like community of a dozen widely-spaced chalets built by and for skiers, particularly ski patrollers. The present owner of the rest of the farm has removed the farm buildings, including the house, in order to avoid paying taxes on buildings he wasn't using until he gets around to building a permanent residence at some future time. Once almost empty of dwellings, Swain Hill road is now lined with cabins and year-round homes.

When the ski area opened, there were 25 houses on Main Street, 16 on Mill Street, and three on "the lane." Today there are 23 houses on Main Street just nine on Mill Street and none on "the lane." This loss of houses has been balanced by two on a new unnamed lane in the space between the Sierra Restaurant and the railroad tracks. Fireside Lane leads to four of the six cabins along Canaseraga Creek. There are also 16 two-storey condos built by the consortium of Livingston, Goins and Gullo and a small motel now converted to two apartments.

In addition to the loss of houses, a total of nine of those remaining now belong to skiers or groups of skiers and are not full-time residences. The demand for housing from skiers and area employees increased the value (and tax assessments) on properties in town, making it advantageous for people to sell and move out of the close-knit community, which some felt was too close-knit, especially as it was confined in a not-very-wide valley. Others, who preferred to remain, have preserved the integrity of the community so that it has not become merely an enclave of mostly absent second-home owners.

The number of cabins and year-round homes up the valley and atop nearby hills keeps growing. Except for the condos and a few cabins, this development has been accomplished by individuals. I have no way of assessing how much of this construction, especially that outside of the hamlet, was influenced by the ski area. It seems to be due more to the overall population increase and a general increase in urban affluence. It can probably be attributed mostly to the natural beauty of the area which inspires people to want to live here or at least acquire a piece of it for themselves where they can perhaps retire in the years to come.

Like all other developments, it cuts two ways. It raises the tax base and restores abandoned farm land to residential use but at the same time converts pieces of the wildness, that attracted many of the new residents to begin with, into mowed replicas of suburbia. This type of development has helped share the country's general prosperity with an economically poor area as landowners benefited from selling land they weren't using and providing more people to share the tax burden.

Perhaps the greatest benefit from the ski area itself to the surrounding area as a whole has been the creation of various types of employment whether outdoor, indoor, mechanical, retail, clerical, or food service related. Almost anyone you talk to in the area has worked at the ski area in some capacity at some time. Paychecks have helped to pay a lot of bills, as well as college tuition, home improvements and no doubt a lot of unnecessary extras. I always smile when I hear campaigning politicians promise to create jobs when, outside of their office staff, they are not the ones who actually do so. While they can in some cases vote for conditions that sponsor job creation, often at taxpayer expense, their promises seem more like convincing the public to vote for them because they will be handing out paychecks.

You can't stop progress. For better or worse, the ski area brought about changes we had not foreseen. The same thing happened at Canandaigua Lake. It was a shock in the summer of 2006 to find an empty space where Aunt Nell's comfortable shingled cottage had once stood. There is nothing left but smoothed-over bare ground and a garage built by a subsequent owner. The people who sold it tried to avoid this happening by stipulating that the cottage was to remain, but the people who bought it almost immediately sold it a third party to whom the restrictions apparently did not apply.

Land there is so expensive that people who can afford to build grander vacation homes are buying up all the simple traditional cottages and replacing them with palatial ones. Progress is generally advantageous, but there is usually a price to pay in the loss of historical structures and local character to say nothing of traditions and individual feelings and higher taxes. What some see as progress others see as destruction. It is happening almost everywhere as it always has done and will no doubt always continue to do.

ROCHESTER TIMES-UNION Fri., Feb. 24, 1956 — *Skiing* — By BILL VANDERSCHMIDT

Challice Robinson Leads Younger Set

A year ago Challice Robinson had trouble standing up. Now she's skiing.

There may be younger enthusiasts than Challice, 2-year-old daughter of Mr. and Mrs. David Robinson who operate the popular Swain Ski Slopes south of Nunda on Route 408, but they're in hiding so far.

Not only does Challice come down the snow covered slopes as frequently and regularly as any other patron of the wax and hickory art, but she even manages to hang onto the tow rope on the way up.

Her skis are three-foot models, cut down from an old pair of seven-footers, and her bindings consist of an old pair of her mother's boots, cut off near the ankles and nailed to the skis.

Mrs. Robinson, herself an accomplished skier, recommends these improvised bindings for the very young. She says youngsters in the 2- and 3-year-old class are apt to become discouraged by the fuss connected with more complicated bindings. With these, it's just a matter of stepping in, overshoes and all.

Little Challice rides up the tow for beginners' slope, with her mother's help, and skis down, also with some moral and physical support from mom.

The Swain beginners' slope is a favorite spot for many small fry while their elders are using the higher, steeper areas, but little Miss Robinson probably holds the record as the most youthful of the half pint set.

She was born on Groundhog's Day in 1954 when her parents were probably hoping, along with other members of the skiing fraternity, that Mr. Groundhog would see his shadow and give them six more weeks at their favorite sport.

YOUNGEST SKIER? — Challice Robinson, 2-year-old daughter of the David Robinsons, operators of Swain Ski Slopes, is probably area's youngest enthusiast.

Restoration by Ariel Robinson

My Chapter

Challice Binless Robinson

The news of their impending parenthood was not an unalloyed joy for Bina and Dave. They were not planning on children just yet because and they needed both salaries to finance the business. Mom's pregnancy did not stop her from skiing, however. She even skied two days before I was born on the second of February, 1954. A Groundhog Day baby might have seemed like a good omen for the ski area but there was, in fact, no more skiing that year.

My debut on the snow came in the 1955-56 season. Equipment for small children was nonexistent in those days so my skis, a pair of seven footers cut down to two and a half feet, had the bottom part of an old pair of rubber boots nailed to them and my snow boots fit inside the adult boots. Mom would take me up the rope tow and down the slope between her skis. I still have those skis. All four of us learned to ski on them, then they kicked around rentals for years. Joe Scott put a pair of cable bindings on them and his kids used them for short skis. One of them lost a tip in my house fire, the bitterest part of the whole loss for me with the exception of Alexander, the cat.

My second pair of skis were sort of striped in orange and silver with an R on one and an L on the other. I knew the R stood for Robinson, but I was a little puzzled about the L. I finally decided it was for one of the L's in Challice. It seemed a funny way of doing it, but adults were doing incomprehensible things most of the time anyway. I'm still not very clear on the difference between right and left.[28]

I used to hang around the bottom of the slopes with my skis on, and Mom and Dad would take me up when they had time. My first solo run occurred when Gail Clark noticed me standing by the beginner lift and very kindly took me to the top. I had never skied without being inside the V of someone else's skis and very quickly lost my balance becoming the center of a big white cloud. When it dissipated, I had one ski on and the other was on its way to the bottom of the hill. Not knowing enough to take the other ski off, I somehow made it down on one ski and one boot. Dad came along and found me at the bottom trying to put my ski back on. He scraped about eight inches of snow from the bottom of my boot and the ski went on.

A girl who was a little older than I kindly showed me how to ride the small rope tow at the edge of Novice slope. "You wait," she said," for the sugar." She meant the splice, because it was fatter than the rest of the rope and easier to hang on to. My parents, busy with the area, found this out when my mittens showed signs of wear from the rope. The big rope tow was a lot more difficult. It was heavier, too heavy for a child to hold up and it went a lot faster, so I would wait at the bottom for someone to take me up. Occasionally the memory of what happened

---

[28] I am sure that the tendency of children to draw conclusions based on their own (limited) experience has amused many parents. My own daughter Ariel refused to ride the chairlift because she saw it went up (and up and up) and thought you had to jump off.

the last time would wear off and I would try to go up by myself. I would make it about ten feet and get thrown off into the bushes to the left every time. My recollection is that those bushes where exceedingly thorny and difficult to get out of.

Jean and I took numerous lessons from Helen DeWolfe who taught the beginners. After a few lessons someone tried to put us in a more advanced class, but we were having none of that. We wanted Helen and with Helen we stayed. She was very kind to us, the weekend orphans. We were around one day when she and Bill were having lunch. She fed us and was concerned that we should have something to drink with the meal (The adults must have been having something unsuitable for children.) so she rooted around until she found a can of juice for us. I was amazed that someone would go to that much trouble for us because we weren't accustomed to getting that much attention.

The Ski Patrol and the cafeteria ladies were also very kind to us, especially Lucille Tucker who was wonderful. We would stay at her farm when Mom and Dad were at trade shows and have a ball with her children, Paul, Kevin and Karen. Helping her husband, Lester, clean the cow barn was considered a high treat. ("Hurry up, kids, they're catching up with us.") The upstairs of their house was unheated, so she would put us to bed under piles of handmade quilts. I loved to read in bed and Lucille tied a string to the lamp cord so I could turn it off without getting out of bed. I think that was the most spoiled I ever felt in my life. Lucille, a natural mother, adopted her children, and when Kevin and Karen found out years later that they had seventeen brothers and sisters, I knew she would not feel the anxiety common to many an adoptive parent at this time. She just felt that she had seventeen more children.

In the early days, we stayed in our old house only on weekends. All us kids slept in one room downstairs. Another crib was added with each successive baby until we were up to four. I remember the excruciatingly cold seat of the chemical toilet, sort of a modern marvel for that place and time, the old wood fired kitchen range and the marvelous texture of the linoleum floor created by the hobnailed boots of a former tenant. When we moved down permanently about 1958 or '59, I was shocked that Mom wanted to replace the floor and paint over the lovely roses on the living room wallpaper. A remnant of the roses remained underneath the bathroom counter. I looked at them ten years later, and they were truly hideous. We spent the first summer sleeping in the house and living in the base lodge. We would walk the dewy path in between in our bare feet. There was a thistle in one spot that always seemed to be where you met someone coming the other way. Baths were achieved in the laundry sink. How poor mother coped with laundry with two in diapers, I don't remember, but it couldn't have been fun.

When the Clark T-bar went in, my troubles were not over. I didn't have enough weight to hold the bar down and would lose it before the first tower. This necessitated a lot of waiting at the end of the lift line for someone to ride up with. The wait was longer because I was too shy to ask if people were single. They had to ask me first and sometimes they would say, "Are you waiting for someone?" and I would confine my reply to "No." If they didn't take the next step and say, "Do you want to ride up with me" I would wait and wait. It surely was a long vigil for a fast ride down. I liked to go fast and my unwaxed wooden skis did not, so I just went straight in order to achieve maximum velocity. Eventually the weight came on, and the wait was over. As I gained proficiency, riding the lift became a piece of cake. Bob Stevens would make it more interesting by holding the T-Bar back until the spring stretched all the way out. He weighed about 130 pounds soaking wet, so he would slide along behind me teeth bared, lower jaw thrust out, until the spring was fully extended. Then he would let go, and I would go flying, first with the t-bar pushing me ahead then pulling the t-bar behind me. I ended up even with the T-bar just at the spot where I used to fall off. I then had a second to get situated before the hill started at the first tower.

Skiing out of the tracks was strictly forbidden and we would not have dreamed of skiing out of the tracks. We might however, in our teens, have thought it was the height of cool to let the outside ski drop back with the tail behind our backs and the tip dragging in the snow along the edge of the tracks. I don't think this ever resulted in a fall, and fortunately skis were much longer then. In later years a shorter ski might have wound up in an extremely uncomfortable place if we had happened to fall on it.

About this time we invented what we then called T-bar tag. In reality it was an earlier version of a quad. We would get part way up the hill, past the first steep part, out of sight of retribution from the lift attendants, and one of us would slip off the t-bar. We kept the inner ski straight in the track the outer one in herringbone position to prevent backward slippage, while our confederates behind us slipped their outer ski between our skis and off we went together. I think Jean and I invented this one day when three of us wanted to ride up together. It worked just as well with four. We just waited until one person was safely established before the next one dropped back. Hard as it may be to believe, there were no terrible accidents involving lacerations, multiple fractures, or multiple ambulance trips. Looking back, it must have taken a lot of dexterity, but we did it as a matter of course. T-bar tag, by the way, explains the mystery of how tower five at the top of the little lift came to have a 15 degree bend in it. Five people, four of whom shall remain nameless in case the statute of limitations has not yet expired, and Michelle May[29] were going up the novice lift, known locally as "the little tow." This lift had t-bars without springs, much easier for beginners to ride, but it also meant that when the four nameless people and Michelle came up against a monstrous bump in the lift path there was no give in the t-bar and there they stuck until the tower bent, which must have taken an amazing amount of force. I would not dare to mention this incident or my contribution to the cause if Dad were still alive.

Those springless t-bars were nice to swing on in the summer. After Dad found out that we were swinging on them, he forbade it. One day, being half way up the hill, I figured it would be safe to swing, but I reckoned without Newton's Third Law of Motion. The movement gradually worked down the hill until Dad saw it and came to administer justice.

I taught Killy, a border collie, to ride piggyback. She thought it pretty cool to come down the hill on my back, clinging to my shoulders, looking like a furry backpack.

The footings for the lifts were dug by hand, and I remember walking up the hill with Dad to find Dick Blowers almost waist deep in the hole

---

[29] Michelle is mentioned due to the fact that when I was 18, the legal drinking age at that time, I bought a six-pack of Maximus Super (a then powerful beer, all of 5% alcohol, I believe) for Michelle at her request. She and others consumed it under the lilacs behind Kerr's store. When my sister Janet found her in an intoxicated state, she asked in horror, "Michelle, who gave you the beer?" Michelle replied, "I can't tell you. I promised I wouldn't get Challice in trouble." Twenty years later, after they had been my lilacs for 17 years and Maximus Super had been extinct for some time, I found one of the cans, probably a valuable collector's item at that point.

for the third tower of the little lift. He had just come across a rock, and told Dad "Look at that, Dave, that's bluestone."

The lift shacks were cool places to hang out in summer smelling of grease and littered with pieces of robin's egg shell. If I could turn back time for just one hour, I'd pick one in the summer. The area was a magical play ground for young children. Mom read us Thornton W. Burgess and I was sure Old Mother West Wind lived atop Rattlesnake Hill letting her Merry Little Breezes loose to play in the meadow between our house and the bottom of the hill. Johnny Chuck lived half way up Old Main, and Grandfather Frog lived in The Stream at the bottom of the hill between Chute and Old Main. The Stream ran along the base of the hill and was covered at the bottom of each trail by whatever material had been handy at the time, varying from two different kinds of railroad ties to slabwood, a little precarious to walk on.

There was a cluster of sumacs atop an old stone pile. The fescue around it looked like green sea waves and the sumac could easily be palm trees creating a Pirate Island. The base of an old kerosene lamp when filled with stream water and fescue brewed sassafras tea, which we miraculously had enough sense not to drink. A witch lived behind the red door and leaf shaped hinges of the patrol building, where she would make a soufflé (pronounced soo-ful) out of you if you weren't careful.

The whole hill became our play ground as we got older, and I knew where all the thistles were because of my habit of running around barefoot. If you walked on the outsides of your feet avoiding too much pressure on your arches, the thistles weren't too bad.

The very heart of the area, to me, was the old snowmaking pond, which you reached from the top of the novice lift. This was a semicircular area cut into the hill and carpeted with moss called by us for no good reason at all Injun Land. The pond was small but absolutely perfect; cattails, peepers, chugarum frogs, and newts. I loved sitting on the rocky verge and listening to the frogs.

One of the Patrollers once said nostalgically, "Remember the old days when Dave ran the outside, Bina ran the inside and the kids picked rocks?" And pick rocks we did, hundreds and thousands of them, solo and chorus, as directed, or because we saw one. It was a given, see a rock pick it up, chuck it over the edge of the trail. It's still almost impossible to pass one by. Usually this was unpaid labor, but on one occasion, faced with what looked more like a shale outcropping than a ski trail a pay scale was temporarily instituted. Years later, this gave me a good comeback when dad was talking about the paucity of his early wages: "So? I picked rocks for a penny a bucket!"

At about the age of five I was capable of picking up cafeteria trays, and at about seven I started washing them also. When old enough to reach the cafeteria counter, I would keep filling up cups of pop for the customers to grab. Probably by eleven I could run the cash register. This involved adding up the total in your head and ringing it up on the register. A piece of scrap paper was used for big orders.

I also worked in rentals, handing out boots adjusting cable bindings etc. There were two pianos downstairs which we used to "play" i.e.; bang on as loud as possible. Joe Scott had enough of that one day and screwed the lids down.

Jean and I started working in the ski shop when we were 13 or so. We went to a couple of trade shows in New York City with Mom and Dad. Trade shows were later held in Las Vegas. A hotel receptionist heard Mom say she wasn't going to gamble and gave her a roll of nickels. A true Scotswoman, Mom took the roll of nickels home with her. Another time she saw a penny in the lift path when we were riding up together and tried to pick it up on the fly. We fell, but she got the penny.

Those are two of my favorite Mom stories but I think the best is one that Siney Spike told me. In the days when the slopes were packed by side stepping, Ky came home visibly drooping. He said "We did Brewer and we did Novice and we did Pines, and she looked at the sky and said 'There's still time to do 80 Acres before dark.' That woman doesn't know when she's done a day's work!" This is what made the business viable, a lot of hard work and a tight rein on the purse strings.

In the fall of 1975 Andrew was involved in a bad accident. Canaserasa Rescue Squad volunteers took turns manually operating their breathing equipment all the way to Rochester to keep him alive. The prognosis wasn't good and Mom and Dad went up to be with him while Jean and I stayed home to open the ski shop. It seems incredible, looking back, that we wouldn't have said to heck with the ski shop and gone to be with our brother, but we didn't even think about it. The area came first. However several people had heard about the accident and came to the rescue. Dean and Melanie Kingsbury were two of them, along with Clarence Nichols, Del Neary, and Dave Miller. There was at least one more, I wish I could remember who, because this still warms the cockles of my heart today. When we got to Rochester, Andrew had regained consciousness and made a speedy recovery.

Growing up on the Ski Slopes

Jeanie Robinson-Pownall

I remember going to the rope tow and waiting at the front of the line for someone to offer to take me up. "You want to go up, Jeanie?" someone would ask. I would nod (often without looking up to see who it was) and climb in front, between his or her skis and hang onto the person's legs for the ride up the hill. I remember Gwennie Underwood, who was tall, slender, and glamorous in cream-colored stretch paths, was always particularly kind and would chat to me on the way up. When I was about 12 the first pair of ski pants I selected for myself were cream like Gwennie's.

Eunice Gaby prepared some of the food for the cafeteria in the kitchen in our home, and I liked to help. We tore wax paper into squares and put an ice cream scoop of hamburger topped with a second square of wax paper on each scoop of hamburger. We then pressed them with a dinner plate. The sandwiches always looked so good ~ Mom devised a system of wrapping them with plastic wrap with an extra fold on top that held two dill pickle slices. Chili was made on our kitchen stove.

The chili was very popular: spicy and thick. Mom made up the recipe, and it included burgundy wine. This was a minor scandal and caused quite a few whispers among the townspeople.

In many ways it was an enchanted childhood. On Friday evenings I would ask my father if we were skiing the next day, and a "yes" produced a euphoric feeling. (Remember, this was before snowmaking.) I used to lay my ski clothes out at the foot of my bed and try to go to sleep early so I could be up at the crack of dawn. Invariably I tossed and turned because I went to bed too early, and would wake up with my clothing wrinkled on the floor and never quite make it to the lifts before they opened.

My father packed the ski slopes at night when the area was closed, and had to snatch his sleep when he could during the day. Once someone asked me what my father did for work and I replied, "He doesn't work, he just sleeps on the couch." No one worked harder, and I made him sound like a lazy bum.

The peak lunch time is 12:00 to 2:00, and Mom did not want to hire someone for a whole or half day when the extra set of hands was needed for just those two hours. She scheduled the four of us to work one hour each on either Saturday or Sunday, collecting, emptying, and washing trays. We didn't like it because that two hour time period was the best time to be on the slopes (while most of the skiers were in the lodge). I remember it certainly wasn't worth getting out of my ski clothes for just an hour, and I quickly learned that slightly-damp leather boots became cold as soon as I went back out skiing. So, I tromped around the base ledge, boot buckles clanging, with a long apron over my expensive Icelandic ski sweater, knickers, and knicker-socks. Not just any apron, mind you, but a long ruffled apron of blue and pink flowers that I had purchased at a church rummage sale. The skiers were too polite to laugh at me (at least to my face), but the town kids were not restricted by any such scruples.

Frozen granular snow has always been my favorite surface and "spring skiing" my favorite time. It was bittersweet because I knew I wouldn't be skiing and seeing friends until the following November or December, but the weather was so beautiful and I savored every lungful of air. First, I could get rid of my bulky and unflattering warm-up pants, and later in the day I would ditch my parka. The Winter Carnival, started by Robin Smith, was greatly anticipated. People wore costumes and there were fun races and silly contests and prizes. I made myself a sunny yellow and black striped tiger suit from fake fur, and it became my trademark costume and (much later) a Halloween costume for my daughter.

Back in those days people were more responsible for their actions and choices than they are today, and liability was not such a big issue. The ski slopes gave away free beer during the Winter Carnival, not only at the bottom but at the top of the hill as well. A few would always over-indulge and we (as) children were greatly amused at their antics and lack of coordination. Drunks were not a scary thing for us because we had a local man who was so shy he wouldn't look anyone in the eye when sober but went around with a big smirk and a cheery word for everyone when he had been tippling. Nowadays people recognize alcoholism as an addiction and a disease and get help for people like Lawrence, but back then it was viewed more as foolish behavior and we liked him just fine the way he was.

Lucille Tucker, the mainstay of the kitchen crew, is the first person who springs to mind when I think of the true Christian spirit. I know this is a cliché, but she was our Sunday school teacher in the little Swain United Methodist Church. She baked luscious chocolate cupcakes with white icing (a recipe from Mother's sister, thus called "Auntie Betty's Chocolate Cake"). They cost 10 cents. Great big oranges and shiny Red Delicious Apples were a quarter- the Red Delicious don't have a lot of flavor but they certainly look appetizing and sold better than other less-showy types.

One day a grease fire flared up on the grill, and Mother and I, working in the ski shop, heard screams from the cafeteria crew. Mother flew behind the counter and hit the big red button and an enormous quantity of baking soda-like stuff poured down onto the grill (as it was supposed to) and all over everything else (a side effect). It was then she saw Lucille, who had calmly readied the fire extinguisher. The grill was four inches deep in powder and the next man in line stepped up and said, "Two cheeseburgers, please." When skiers come inside they want to eat and get back on the slopes and a little thing like a fire and billowing baking soda wasn't going to stop him. (As it turned out the fire was minor and the fire extinguisher would have been a better choice and a lot easier to clean up, but there was a lot of smoke and it looked pretty scary.)

Our next door neighbors Barb and Ted Swain sold lift tickets in the ticket booth, and Barb worked in the ski shop as well. Both had a great sense of humor and distinctive laughs. I remember Ted telling the story of a man who stomped right into the lodge with his skis on; he apparently had difficulty getting them on and did not want to remove them just to come into the lodge. Another story was about the man who rented skis, bought a lift ticket, and then came inside and asked how much more it would have cost to use the lifts instead of side-stepping up the hill. Barb and Ted's son Shawn, an only child, is our "fifth sibling" and still keeps skis and boots at Challice's house for when he is in town from his home in Arizona.

Marilyn Weidman, another close neighbor, ran her own licensed beauty shop in part of her house. She was glamorous and "with it" and good to talk with during those rough teenage years. I would float something by her to get her reaction before springing it on my parents.

When I was 15, I was hired by the ski school and began teaching. Being a ski instructor is considered glamorous, and I must admit that was probably part of the attraction. Swain had a very large high school and college group program, and I taught several nights a week. I worked in the ski shop with Mom on the weekends, and invariably some of my students would drift in to say hello. For some reason some very shy boys showed an interest, and I became good at making conversation and making them feel at ease, an attribute that has helped me considerably in life.

There was a tragedy in 1975 when two of my cohorts from the ski school, David "Wheels" Wagenblass and Glenn Lapham were killed in a car crash on their way to dinner. Wheels had an adorable pale yellow VW bug painted in 1970's fashion with turquoise lace which I dubbed "the Easter egg." Wheels and Glenn drove up behind a farm tractor that had rear positioned "headlights" pointing at them, and Wheels was blinded or momentarily became confused as to which half of the road was his. He crossed the center line, and they were struck by a large car and died at the scene. Years later Glenn's date for the evening, Marty Halbert from Canaseraga, a friend and classmate of mine I had introduced him to, told me how she had waited and waited for him, thinking he had been detained at the ski school.

Glenn, who had a speech impediment except when he was teaching, was very shy and used to come into the ski shop and smile at me but not say much. I used to make mental notes during the day so I would have something to tell him, and I found myself still saving up tidbits for him a year after he had died. Each has a trail named after him; Glenn was the racer so the racing slope was re-named "Glenn's Run" and a parallel trail was re-named "Wheels' Run." Beautiful, special signs were made by Ken Moffatt, and he took care to make the signs of identical size. One summer the maintenance crew took the signs down to re-stain them, and when they put them back up they mixed them up. Soon the maps were printed with the error, and the racing slope is "Wheels" to this day. I often think of Wheels and Glenn, frozen in time, at the peak of their physical perfection in their 20's; and every time I am on the racing slope I send a thought to Glenn that I know it is really his slope.

The ski center exposed us to a very diverse group of people. Chic Carlucci, the assistant director of the ski school, is a character worth noting. Flirtatious in the polite European sense, charming, suave and gentlemanly, Chic (pronounced "Chick") is one of my very favorite Swain people. He provided stability and considerable élan to the ski school. He and his wife Joanie, also a ski instructor, started their two children skiing at a young age. The navy blue with narrow orange striped Fischer felt hats were very popular with the ski school; not only were they stylish and warm but the colors matched the ski school parkas. Brian and Karen wore the same hats as their parents but with a different effect: the adult-sized hats were so tall on their little bodies that it gave a "Cat in the Hat" effect. They were both sweet, indulged but not spoiled, and adorable.

One of my early students was AJ Kitt, who would later become a four time Olympian in the downhill and super-giant slalom. Both of AJ's parents, Nancy and Ross, were ski school instructors. They would send AJ along in some of my classes (probably so they could get some skiing in without him). He was always a good-natured little kid but did not want to be stuck in lessons and he used to take off and bomb down the hill, giving me a big grin over his shoulder. There was nothing I could do about it because I had other (paying) students in the class and couldn't chase after him. With no help from me, AJ is now listed in the United States Ski Hall of Fame, the only American man to ski in four consecutive Olympics and the winner of several World Cup medals before he retired from racing.

Robin Smith eventually came to run the whole ski center, but apparently his "full speed ahead, damn the torpedoes" management style that served all of us so well on the ski school was not compatible with running the entire area, and he went bankrupt, leaving my parents, who had worked so hard and were so frugal for all those years, as his biggest creditors. We were very thankful when a consortium led by Phil Saunders purchased the area from the Bank of Castile; otherwise, it might have closed and we wouldn't have had anywhere to ski.

I had always said I would get married on the Ski Slopes, imagining myself in a long white lacey gown with my big Lange ski boots sticking out the bottom and the veil streaming out behind me as I skied fast. I didn't manage that, but having an August wedding did not stop me from getting married on the slopes. My husband Jim and I were

Dave and Bina Robinson

married in 1980 on the little beginner hill where I gave so many people their first lessons. Much later, I worked with our own children, Jenny and Jamie, on the same familiar ground.

Andy's Recollections

Andrew McLeod Robinson

Son Andy has to do things his own way. After ignoring my requests for information, he presented me with a tape of verbal recollections. I have just finished listening to it. With hair still standing on end, I'll set down some of the highlights.

I remember when we first came to Swain, we slept in the base lodge. It was cold in the morning and Mother made us scrambled eggs in a big cast iron frying pan and served them to us in little blue bowls with white specks. We called them the snow flake bowls, and Mom said "Hope for a lot of snow this winter, kids." It was a big move for Mom and Dad. They had sold their house in Honeoye Falls and had come down to run the ski area full time with four young kids.

We were pretty lucky. We got to ski a lot. There was an awful lot of work to do. We used to come home from school on Friday night and stand in assembly line where one child would put an ice cream scoop of hamburger on a square of wax paper. The next child would top it with another square of wax paper and press it down with a plate. The next child would pack it in a box. We'd do 200 hamburgers for a Saturday.

Mixing salads in great big stainless steel bowls with a huge spoon that was like a shovel for a little kid.

We used to answer the phone and give out ski reports. We used to do it in shifts, maybe every two hours or something like that. That sucked when there was nice skiing out because you had to sit in there and answer the phone for a couple of hours.[30] One time I left the phone unattended. Dad made me stay in for the next two weekends. No skiing because I had to answer the phone all weekend.

I barely remember the rope tows except for riding with Dad leaning back against his legs to get up the hill. I don't remember the Clark T-bar being installed, but I remember it being there. It had a 392 Industrial Chrysler Hemi motor. The guys put thrush mufflers on it and it sounded like a drag strip.

Every bull wheel has a dog on it to keep it from going backwards if it should shut down. Each has its own thump to it. The 80-Acre lift went tumptatatumptump.[31] The one on Clark just went tumptadatump. I remember years later riding up a Hall T-bar at Toggenburg. I was looking at the lift towers. They were painted black, but I noticed some blue paint showing through and some red paint showing through on the sheaves. Still out of sight of the bull wheel, I heard tumptatatumptump.

---

[30] Challice: "I don't remember having to give up skiing to answer the phones. There must have been times when individual kids were on call for this, though, because I do remember being in the bath tub and being told to remove myself because I was on phone duty despite my protests that I could very well get out of the tub to answer the phone. Eunice would have been there to answer the phones on the weekends when the lifts were running."

[31] Janet: "I loved the merry sound the 80 acre lift made. When it was running it would be a busy day with lots of friends to ski with."

I started hooting and hollering. The guy came out of the watchman's shack and I yelled. "Where did you get that lift? Did it come from Swain?" He shook his head. He didn't know. The girl I was riding up the lift with said I was embarrassing her.

When we got older, maybe 15 or 16, we used to get off the school bus on a Friday night and go to work in the rental room. It would be 11 o'clock before we got the rental room closed up and then we'd go right out and make snow, Mitchell May and I. I think I was making like $120 a week when I was 15 years old. I had a TV and stereo in my room that I bought myself.

Making snow was the best job because you got to ride the snowmobiles. Harry and Lyle used to mix up a 5-gallon can of gas because they knew Mitchell and I would go through it. We were out on that hill all night, checking the guns, making good snow, but we rode those snowmobiles all night long. We'd go in the shop, fuel up the compressors and maybe get a cup of coffee. Dad thought we were doing such a good job (which we were) because he heard the snowmobiles all the time.

Sometimes, if someone called in sick, I'd work two shifts and still go to school the next day. I used to go to school smelling like diesel fuel. The farm boys sometimes smelled like cow manure.

Dad used to sleep on the couch. When there was a problem one of the guys would come up to house and ring the doorbell. He'd go out and fix the problem. Sometimes he wouldn't wake up and I'd go out and try to help. Sometimes we'd have to get him up anyway.

As we got older, we used to ride the chairlift and carry the propane tank in case we had to thaw a frozen pipe and walk down to check the snow guns because it was a lot easier than running the snowmobiles up and down. Dave Maul (Heavy) used to sleep in the lift house. One very cold night I opened the door and threw a shovel full of cold snow on Heavy's bare back. He came out of the shack in his boxer shorts and chased me.

I ran around the shack and pulled the door shut so that he was locked out. He headed for his car to get his spare keys, but I headed him off with the snowmobile keeping him from getting to his car. Heavy was about 5'4" and weighed about 400 pounds. Finally he was begging me, "Please, please, I'm freezing." Poor guy. I never should have done it to him.

That Sunday, I was the last man on top and coming down alone on the lift. Heavy stopped the lift right over the snow making pond. He must have made 50 or 60 iced snowballs. He could throw hard and probably hit me with 20 of them. It hurt. I never messed with him after that.

I remember when Harry Weaver came to the door and asked for a job. I asked Dad if he was going to hire him. He answered, "He's a veteran. I'll give him a job any time."

The 80-Acre T-bar was the newest one at the slopes. That was "my" lift. I had to start it up at noon, 11 o'clock if it was really busy, on Saturday and Sunday. I'd take a Tucker SnoCat or the Bombardier and two other guys. It was a really fast T-bar. There were never any problems because it was new.

One day the bombardier caught fire. We threw shovelfuls of snow on it. Got it out and got it down the hill OK.

When you were at the top of a lift, you were up there all day. The ski patrol or somebody would bring you lunch. I hated mustard. I made the mistake of asking not to have any mustard on my lunch. After that, my lunch used to have mustard on the French fries, mustard on the hot dog, mustard in the potato chips, even mustard in my pop. I never should have told them I didn't like mustard. I was the boss's son. It was a way to get even with the boss.[32]

Barb and Ted Swain used to sell tickets in the base lodge. You could always smell Ted's pipe when you walked into the base lodge in the morning. When he sneezed, it would wake the dead. Phil Isaman used to sell tickets and run rentals and repairs. I think that was at the bottom of one of the rope tows.

We skied so much as children, we'd wake up at night with cramps in our legs. Oh, they would hurt. Dad would hear us moaning and come in and hold your calf with those great big hands of his and get the cramp out. We each had a heating pad, but it seemed that Dad was always right there. He probably didn't sleep well because there was so much money in the house. I can remember going into his upstairs office once to ask him about something and he was sitting on the bed counting money and there were piles and piles of money around. He said, "Don't you tell anybody what you saw in here." He was pretty upset that I'd walked in without an invitation to enter.

---

[32] Jeanie: "Challice and I are very doubtful that putting mustard into Andy's food had anything to do with getting even with the boss. Please refer to the incident of shutting Heavy out in the cold in his underwear and the mudball slinging at Roger elsewhere in Andy's account."

The Novice lift had an International motor and the Brewer T-bar a Continental. They had to be started with cranks. I was so little I had to jump on the lever. One day it was cold, way below zero, 20 below or lower. The Novice lift wouldn't start. There were 4 or 5 guys standing around doing nothing while I was trying to jump on the lever to start it. So here comes Dad. He chewed everybody's butt because I was the only one doing any work. He shook my hand and said, "You can come and work for me any time when you get old enough."

"Get back!" he warned and grabbed hold of that lever and rolled that motor over 10 or 15 times as hard and fast as he could because he was mad. It fired right up and started. He pulled the crank out and threw it down "You are all half my age and ought to be able to turn that motor over," he grumped and stormed off.[33]

There was a guy named Bill Jenkins. I'm not sure how he got involved. We used to have to prime the Ford Industrial motor on a water pump. The guys welded an H pipe on it and put some big mufflers on it and boy, did that thing talk. We had a 6" water line from the pond that we had to prime using an old hand-operated vacuum pump through a 3/8" tube pushed up on to that 6" pipe. It would take two men pumping as hard as they could. There were no two men who could accomplish the entire task. You kept having to switch off. Only Lyle Weaver could hang right in there and do it. You'd pump as long as you could, two minutes maybe, then someone else would take over. It would take 15

---

[33] Challice recalls hearing a similar story from several witnesses: "There were that about three or four people were trying to get it to crank over, one was Mitch May and maybe Rod Swain. Dad came in to see what the hold up was and said 'Gads, boys, gads' and cranked it over by himself in two seconds flat. This was the basis for the legend of how incredibly strong Dad was, something I believed implicitly for years until someone pointed out at that none of these employees was very old or strong at that time."

minutes to get that thing to pump. All of a sudden, it wouldn't pump any more and they'd throw the clutch on motor and she'd take off. Sometimes it didn't start and you'd have to start all over again. Jenkins came down with an old vacuum pump from a milking system that made it a lot easier.

I remember once Don Butler was cranking something over by hand, maybe the old welder. Something kicked back and barked his knuckles badly, might even have broken a finger or two, He took the crank out and threw it. Lucky thing the window was open because it went right through the window opening and landed on the snowmaking pond. I was the lightest one there and had to go out on the ice and get it.

Spring carnival used to be some time around Easter. We used the Thiokol to dig a hole, lined it with plastic and filled it with water. A jump of piled up snow a little farther uphill gave a skier the chance to jump over the pond - or land in the water. I think you had to be 4 feet tall in order to compete. Greg Swain won it that year. It must have been 30 feet across. He cleared it but broke his binding when he landed.

The event was over with when we happened to look up the hill and saw Calvin Cleland going lickety-split as fast as he could toward the jump. He wasn't tall enough to be in the event, was probably only 3'6" tall. He landed smack dab in the middle. I think it was Harry and Lyle who jumped in and pulled him out of there. Calvin gasping for breath. He went back home, changed his clothes and went right back out skiing again. I can still see that crazy little kid coming down and nailing that jump. It turned out Calvin was mentally ill, poor kid. As a young adult, he took his own life. I'll always remember his bravado taking that jump.

I remember when we were building the Brewer T-bar. We used the old Bombardier to haul lumber for a cement sluice so they could bring cement down for the tower foundations. I was riding on the front. We had just turned to go up the woods road when the pile of lumber fell off. Harry was driving and yanked back on the steering clutch and hit the brakes in time for me to avoid being driven into the lumber, which could have killed me. I was only about 8 years old. Harry was really shaken. He took me down to the office and told Dad he couldn't have me up there any more because of what had almost happened. Dad told me I couldn't ride on the equipment any more. So I walked up there just to hang out with them. Bum cigarettes off them (Horrors! -ed.).[34]

At one time there was a building at the top of Clark Slope with outdoor toilets for men and women. I was so little I couldn't get my skis off so I used to walk up the ramp with my skis on. Sometimes a patroller or instructor would lift me up.

In the spring we kids would ski all day Saturday and Sunday and go to school on Monday with faces sunburned so red, the teacher'd send you to the nurse's office. The nurse would send us home. We'd load our faces up with S5 which Mom used to sell in the ski shop and go skiing all day Monday.

One Saturday, Paul Tucker and I rode up the Clark T-bar and skied down through the pines on Pine Trail. A turkey flew out of a pine tree. One of his wings hit Paul in the head and knocked him down.

One day, must have been a Saturday, when Roger Hess was bulldozing the lift path for the 80- Acre T-bar, a big bunch of us kids went up and threw mud balls at him.

---

[34] Janet: "I remember Dad once absent-mindedly called Andy 'Honey' in front of the guys and Andy heard about it for quite a while."

After telling us to knock it off several times, he got off the bulldozer and chased us. I was the youngest one. He caught me, grabbed a stick and whaled my butt until I cried. I didn't tell Dad because I was afraid I'd get it again. Rog told Dad. I didn't get it again, but I got a good talking to.

After you'd make a new trail, you'd have to pick all the rocks off it. And spread hay on it so the grass would grow. Lyle Weaver could spread hay quicker than anybody I ever saw in my life. He wasn't much older than me. He quit school, went to work at the ski slopes and is still there, does a helluva good job. There's a guy that can weld, fix the lifts. Any maintenance thing, he can take it apart and put it together. All the way from the old Tucker SnoCats up to these new groomers, there's nothing on them he can't fix.

When we were real little, they made Round Top Trail. I can remember being up there 4th of July weekend. Mother and Dad raked the rocks. We children picked up the rocks and put them in gallon paint cans. Dad would come by with a 5 gallon bucket, dump ours into that, carry it to the bank and come back, I think we got paid a nickel for each paint can we filled. I remember Challice made a dollar. She was the oldest. I think I was four and Janet three. Talk about slavery. Then they put us all in the car took us to Canandaigua Lake where we went swimming.

Names I remember: Ski Patrol - Marty Kron,[35] Ray Meyering, Cliff Champion, John and Judy Sherman, Werner Schmidtman, Adam

---

[35] Jeanie – "Andy used to ski with the Ski Patrol and Marty Kron gave him an old "pack" - a belt bag with first aid supplies. By then the patrol packs were blue with a bright yellow cross. The older one Marty gave Andy was black with a white cross. He was very proud to ski with the Ski Patrol."

Adams, Ernie Brown, Harry Stoneham, and Glenn Austin, among others.

The first time I was in a SnoCat, I might have been five. In the middle of middle Brewer there used to be a maple tree. Dad was packing the slope and cut in close to that maple tree. There must have been a lot of snow drifted in behind it, and he damn near rolled the SnoCat over. I remember I fell over against him because the cat had tipped over so far. It righted itself, but it shook him up. He went down and told the guys he wasn't going to do the grooming any more. And told them not to take me with them.

There used to be a piece of quick sand out behind the old shop. We kids with rubber boots on were playing in it, got stuck, somebody ran and got Eunice. She got Rog Hess who married Gerry Spike. Roger dug us out with a shovel. I think he had to get big sheets of plywood to stand on so he didn't sink in. We were up to our waists.[36] If somebody hadn't got help, we probably would have died right there.

---

[36] Challice: "Andrew, just Andrew and only Andrew, was playing in the quicksand. We three girls would never have dreamed of playing in the quick sand because we had been told not to and we were good children with a healthy fear of the heavy hand of the law which in those unenlightened days would have been apt to land hard upon our bottoms. The three sweet and innocent girls were headed up the old road behind the old shop when they heard Satan, I mean Andrew, calling from the quicksand where he had been playing ALL BY HIMSELF. We kindly gave up our walk and went down to rescue him and all of us wound up stuck in the quicksand. Fortunately, slow-sinking mud would have been a better description and our boots were only two or three inches below the surface when Eunice came out of the house and told us to step out of our boots with a rather annoyed air as if we were subnormal mentally not to have thought of it for ourselves. We may have stepped out of the boots into Roger's rescuing arms while he was standing on plywood, but all I remember is that he was given the job of retrieving our abandoned boots."

Janet's Recollections

Janet Davison Robinson

Since I'm the youngest, I don't have as many memories of the ski slopes in the early days. I am told that I started walking on my 1st birthday while I was watching the side of the house being put back in place. I don't remember living anywhere else.

I do remember being very small - say 2 ½ - and wanting to go out skiing. Eunice helped me put on boots and skis and off I went. I wasn't sure if I was allowed to go up the lifts so I spent most of a day going down to the Clark lift and watching people getting on and then I would go up to the Novice lift and watch there. I really wanted to go too, but didn't know how to go about it. I just kept going back and forth between the two lifts. Dad came along on skis - must have been a slow day - and asked me if I wanted to go up. Ah! Yes, I did. I watched carefully as we got to the top and saw people sliding off the T-bars and I did the same. I headed down behind them - I remember Dad asking me if I knew what to do, but I was already gone. I spent the rest of the day riding up and going straight down. It was fun. I would sit down at the bottom to stop myself.

The next day I noticed that other people turned as they came down. It may have been triggered by people shouting in surprise as I ran over the fronts or backs of their skis on my way down. Skis were very long in those days, so that's not quite so bad as it sounds. So I tried turning too. It worked!

I do remember picking rocks for a nickel a bucket as Andy tells about. It was a pretty big bucket to a little girl and it seemed like a lot of work for small return. But there was always work to be done and we all pitched in. I liked helping Eunice in our kitchen pressing scoops of hamburger into patties with plates. Later, when I was older I remember pitching in running the cash register in the kitchen to free up one of the ladies to cook during the busy lunch time. I loved those old gold filigreed registers. Carrying trays down from the upstairs of the ski barn was a lot harder in ski boots, but I didn't want to lose the time changing out of them. I fell down the stairs a few times with a pile of trays.

The mailing list was always a huge project. Collating lists, alphabetizing and labeling; it would seem like we would never get the kitchen table back! We had a mimeograph for the early newsletters and Mom would turn the handle thump, thump, and out the purplish slightly stinky papers would come.

The ski barn before the addition was pretty sweet. A wall of windows to see out of while you sat and ate upstairs, the kitchen and ski shop on the ground floor and downstairs, rentals/ski repairs and the fire. It was a nice place to get cozy and warm. The smell of P-tex always makes me think of Joe Scott and LaVerne Wirt, who were busy working in the back room. A favorite pastime was to find discarded cups and place a paper one outside of a styrofoam cup and toss it in the fire. The styrofoam would distort into interesting shapes but it was over quickly, so you would have to find another set to watch again.

When Dad built the addition, there was lots of seating at the ground level (again with nice windows) and the upstairs became more for storage. But the old wall of windows was still there, with the lovely weathered barn boards. I remember going upstairs once years ago, after the latest addition and there was nothing left of the old barn but one beam running across on the stairway. It moved me to tears that the beam was all that was left. It does now just thinking about it.

Lula Griffith usually ran the little sandwich and soda counter in what is now the Shawmut room. I liked helping her out when it was busy. The sandwiches wrapped with a pickle slice, the big stainless milk dispensers, bags of chips, apples, oranges and soda pop. I got pretty good at reaching around and hooking up a new soda canister when one was empty. I would tell my friends who were buying a big cup of pop that 2 smalls for 30 cents was better deal than a large for a quarter.

Barb and Ted Swain have both passed on now and I always see them in my mind's eye at the ticket counter. They were so much a part of everything with Ted's booming laugh and Barb's dry wit. We went through many different incarnations of tickets; yellow tear off single rides are the first ones I remember. For a long time, season pass holders got a daily ticket too and it was fun to see how long a multicolored string you could get.

Christmas vacations were such a long lovely stretch. We would ski all day and night and then collapse into bed. I remember once when I fell asleep with my hat on and my hair was in such snarls in the morning

I decided to just put my hat back on and out I went. Nobody knew about my hair for days until someone snatched my hat off. That was embarrassing.

Our dog Killy loved to ski and not just for the attention she got, although she was an attention seeker. We missed being on TV one afternoon when a cameraman showed up unexpectedly to catch us on tape and we were visiting instead of skiing. Herm Auch of the Democrat and Chronicle took some nice pictures though. Killy would get really upset with me if I would put her down in the lift line because she was afraid I would make her run up instead of ride in style on the chairlift. She barked and carried on until I would put her on my back again. It took some adjustments to ski with her, which was good training for years later when Matthew and Bethany were babies and I would take them skiing in a hip sling.

The air compressors for the snow machines were close to the house and very noisy, but in a good way. They made it easy to fall asleep - unless they stopped during the night. Then I think the whole town woke up.

Mom and Dad were so busy during the season that it seems like we hardly saw them. The up side of that was the rest of the year, when they had more time than most parents do. There was always work to be done, but time to relax too.

Skiing is such a nice way to meet people and it was fun to watch friendships build between kids of different communities who might never have met otherwise. Things have changed a lot at Swain over the years, but that's still true.

Potpourri

I could go on recounting the past for the rest of my life, but have to stop writing sometime if this book is ever to see print. Therefore, with my deadline still unmet and more material still surfacing, I'm going to lump some of the items yet to be assimilated into this one chapter and send the lot off to the printer.

Most of the area people, especially those living on farms, in the generation preceding Dave's and mine seemed to have developed a special refinement characterized by a gentle manner. It seemed as if the hustle and bustle of the 20th century hadn't caught up with them and they were not in a rush to catch up with it. Of course they worked hard and fast, sometimes to exhaustion, when necessary but they seemed to have a more relaxed and kindlier attitude toward life in general. This attitude seems to have gradually worn off in succeeding generations as necessity and mainstream economics have caught up with their descendents, but traces of it are still discernible in the attitude and speech of some individuals in their 80's and even younger.

I wanted to make this refinement clear before airing some less-civilized characteristics that emerged from time to time and provided a good source for gossip among those who tended to derive amusement from some of the goings on.

Back in the '40's and '50's, Swain had a drinking problem. At least two, and maybe a couple more people were afflicted with alcoholism, but for the most part it seemed as if some folks, predominately males, looked forward to getting drunk now and then as a form of recreation. A few drinks on a Saturday night sometimes turned into a binge that went on for a week or more or at least until the money to buy more booze ran out.

This was really hard on family members. I am haunted by one sad Dickensian scene of a woman carrying a baby and surrounded by other small children temporarily abandoning her home to a group of her husband's drinking pals as she made her way to a relative's house. It was good to know that she would not for long be at the mercy of the cold wind that was blowing that day.

Drinking also imposed a financial burden on families. I can remember one young boy, when he was just 10 or so, buying shoes for himself and a younger brother when it was time for school to start. The parents were unable to do so because they had recently spent all their money on booze. Instead of spending the money that had been given to him in dimes and quarters to buy pop and potato chips (in lieu of the lunch his mother was not up to cooking) during the summer, this wise young man had saved it for the start of school. He kept it hidden in a jar under his bed so that no one would take it when they ran out of money for booze.

Every once in a while somebody would make a batch of poteen (an Irish whiskey distilled from potatoes) and invite friends to participate in its consumption. Occasions like this were likely to lead to a week-long binge for some of the participants plus a few days of malaise as they recovered from alcohol poisoning. Not surprisingly, there were perhaps an equal number of virtuous teetotalers who couldn't help reveling in their own superiority on these occasions.

This made for an interesting social mix. I can remember one occasion when strong church goers boycotted an elderly minister who had just been appointed by the diocese without seeking their approval. It was then that Dave and some of the poteen imbibers, who did not normally attend church, showed up on Sunday so that the new minister would have someone to preach to. The situation eventually got sorted out somehow and matters returned to normal. I cite the occasion to show that in spite of their ill-advised drinking habits, these were really worthwhile as well as hard-working people and the division between saints and sinners was not always all that clear cut.

Aside from those inflicted with alcoholism, I'm not sure why these folks drank but surmise that boredom and the need for a little excitement may have been responsible for some of it. It was sad when they ran out of money and came to the house, feeling terrible and asking for an advance on their wages. Dave used to give them a couple of bucks out of his pocket, "enough to sober up on" but not enough to prolong the binge.

I can remember Harry Knights who owned and ran the hardware store[37] in Canaseraga telling me about one occasion on which Canaseraga residents derived a lot of amusement from watching folks from Swain leaving the local bar and spending half an hour or more trying to get along the sidewalk and into their cars. Individual members of the group would fall down and others who weren't any steadier on their feet would go back to help them and end up joining them on the sidewalk. This went on until all the topers succeeded in getting into their cars and mercifully reaching home without death or injury.

Everybody was less educated about drunk driving back in those days. Nowadays someone would have the sense to call the state police if rides home could not be arranged, but there were fewer people and cars back then and people had become accustomed to drunkenness whether or not they disapproved of it. I can remember driving home after an evening of dancing at the American Legion on more than one Saturday night when the car ahead of us was weaving from one side of the road

---

[37] Harry's store was an authentic early 1900's hardware store. As soon as you opened the door you could smell the oakum stored on the second floor. In case you don't know what oakum is, it consists of long, loosely twisted strands of jute or hemp fiber impregnated with tar. It is used for stuffing cracks to repel wind and rain. I believe it is also used between the planks to prevent the seams of wooden boats from leaking. I found the odor pleasant. The next thing you noticed were the horse collars hanging from the high ceiling . These were left over from the days when all the field work was literally horse- powered. They eventually disappeared after being bought by the perpetrators of horse pulling contests. Unlike most modern hardware stores where you pick up a packet of screws or bolts closest to the size you want, Harry had every available size in the triangular drawers of a carefully-made octagonal cabinet that rotated on a sturdy base. In winter, the store was heated by a large round oak wood stove. Around the stove were old buggy seats occupied by farmers who had time to visit with each other during the winter months. Harry wore thick glasses but still had very poor vision. He kept track of people's purchases by writing in very large numbers in account books without regard for lines. Carl Saxton, who worked at the bank, would periodically transcribe them on to ledger sheets and send out bills as needed. Sometimes, Harry had to ask customers to read off the price of an item to him.

to the other. It was only moving at something like 15 miles an hour, but we patiently pulled over and waited or crawled behind it rather than risk passing. Sometimes there was a light fall of snow in which the serpentine tire tracks were clearly etched for subsequent motorists to see.

It's a mercy there weren't more accidents, which reminds me of the time that a carload of recreational drinkers left Swain and drove straight across Route 408 (now Route 70) and into the rock cliff at the base of Rattlesnake Hill. There were a couple broken bones on that occasion, but it didn't bring about any noticeable reform. The accident may have been a case of a misdirected foot hitting the accelerator instead of the brake as opposed to not heeding the stop sign.

Alcohol consumption had another drawback: fights. A few perfectly nice people when sober seemed to enjoy getting into fights on Saturday nights. I'm told that a bunch of regular imbibers from Swain would try to start a fight with other customers at Canaseraga's only bar. When they were unable to egg anyone into fighting with them, they would solve the problem by fighting with each other. I suppose there were some black eyes and nosebleeds, but I never heard of anyone being seriously injured.

The next generation either learned from their parents' example or found better ways of amusing themselves. The advent of television provided an incentive to stay home, and everybody (but us for much of the time) had a television set. This reminds me of one weekend when we had just installed a new lift motor that produced an annoying flicker on all the TV sets on Mill Street. We were considerately not informed of the problem until Sunday afternoon and were able to get someone to come in on Monday to fix the problem, a good example of the cooperation we received from our neighbors.

One incident that comes to mind occurred on a windy day when David Maul, who came to us from Buffalo for several winters, was manning the lift attendant's house at the top of the novice lift on Brewer Slope. David, who at his own suggestion was also known as "Heavy," probably weighed close to 400 pounds. He had telephoned a couple of times that he was afraid the wind was going to blow the attendant's house off its foundation, but was told this couldn't happen. The gusts kept getting stronger, however. David's last transmission was a firm "The captain is abandoning ship" just before he was seen hurrying out of the attendant's house. With his weight no longer holding it down, it immediately blew over.

David was well liked and I wish his story had a happier ending. To save money, he was by then camping out in a small portable cabin he had built for the purpose. One morning after he uncharacteristically failed to show up for work, he was found dead in his bed, a victim of heart failure.

It wasn't all tragedy and heroism, however. Donny Johnson, whose maintenance job required getting around the area by snowmobile tells the following story about Clarence Nichols[38]: Clarence, a typical example of the area's kindly, soft-spoken older generation, was a retired

---

[38] Clarence kept half a dozen or so cows and his wife Gertrude kept chickens. Clarence delivered the eggs to various customers along with the butter Gertrude churned from some of the cream that was not shipped to a milk processor. I can remember Gertrude sitting in a rocking chair using the rocking motion to help turn the handle of an old-fashioned, hand-operated churn. After the butter had formed, she would deftly use a wooden paddle to mark each mound of butter with a leaf-like design.

farmer above Garwoods on the other side of the hill. His job at the time was manning an upper chair lift terminal. Usually, he was able to ride up on another lift. For some reason that was not immediately possible on this occasion. Clarence had always taken a very dim view of snowmobiles and preferred to walk as opposed to accepting a ride even on the flat from the base one lift to another. This time, however, Donny persuaded him that it would be more efficient than the alternative of climbing all the way on foot. They set off traveling up Brewer with Clarence sitting behind Donny clutching his metal lunch box to his chest.

All went well until they reached the steep upper headwall at which point Donny describes how he saw Clarence's boots swing past his head in an upward arc. He turned to see Clarence sliding down the slope on his back, feet in the air, still hugging his lunch box. I never talked to Clarence about this, just learned of it in fact, but feel sure the experience confirmed his opinion of snowmobiles and that he never accepted another invitation to ride. The incident may have had something to do with his transferring to a job in the base lodge not too long afterward.

It seems that boys have a greater propensity to play practical jokes than girls. I'm told there was a period when paying attention to business in the maintenance shop involved tricking co-workers into getting grease on their hands. On one occasion, grease was applied out of sight under the door knob to the maintenance building where it would smear the fingers of the next person to enter. As it happened, Dave was that person. I don't recall his mentioning it to me, but I'm told his reaction was to dismiss it as "child's play" to the embarrassment of the perpetrator. If it had happened to me, I should probably have thought it an accident, but Dave, having once been a boy, recognized it for what it was.

This incident was a temporary aberration that belies the serious unrelenting work involved in keeping machines in good operating condition. Besides the increasingly complicated groomers, there are pumps, air compressors, generators, bulldozers, tractors, mowing machines, four wheelers and snowmobiles, in addition to all the elevated lift machinery to be inspected and greased or replaced as needed. The need for maintaining all this equipment has the advantage of providing full-time, year-round jobs for a small number of technically skilled employees as opposed to the need for a larger number of employees during the ski season.

Before our time, Hallowe'en was celebrated the old-fashioned way with tipped over outhouses. Daughter Jeanie recalls hearing of one occasion when the outhouse was moved back a few feet occasioning the next visitor in the dark of night to wind up in the pit. When adults got involved, as they sometimes did, a hay wagon occasionally wound up on a roof. In our time it was mostly just a mess of cornstalks and smashed jack-o'-lanterns and toilet paper wastefully festooned in trees. Once, it was the beautiful yellow mums I had planted that thrived along the west side of the Shawmut room. Fortunately, enough of the roots survived for the plants to recover and bloom again the following year.

As the years passed by, I became less associated with events outside the base lodge even to the extent of becoming almost a non-skier. To demonstrate one of my memory lapses, there was the time a SnoCat rolled over on precipitous Upper Brewer with Harry Weaver inside. I must have known about it at the time because Challice remembers it, but I have no recollection of what must have been a very traumatic event. Although the roof had been pressed almost down to the steering wheel, Harry was unhurt and able to crawl out with the assistance of his brother Lyle, who was driving another SnoCat nearby.

They went down to the office to let Dave know about it, no doubt dreading his reaction which, according to Harry, was: (1) to be assured that Harry wasn't hurt; (2) to ask if they could get the Cat off the slope; and (3) to ask if any oil had been spilled on the snow. The last sounds trivial, almost laughable under the circumstances, but spilled oil could have been detrimental to the performance of the skis of anyone who skied through it. If any oil had been spilled, the area would have had to have been roped off until it was cleaned up.

As it was, no oil was spilled and Harry and Lyle were able to get the Cat out of the way and back to the shop where it could be repaired, the best possible ending to an unhappy event which could have resulted in serious human injury and the loss of a much-needed snow groomer. Bill Jenkins, a Warsaw area farmer who had married Dolores Blakley's sister, Dorine,[39] was general outdoor manager at the time. Under his direction, the roof was raised and the cab fitted with junkyard windshields until it could be properly repaired during the off-season. I'm not sure, but it is not unlikely that, Bill being a farmer, baling wire was involved in the temporary repair.

This incident illustrates that it isn't just skiers and snowboarders who perform out of the ordinary feats at ski areas. Working on lifts and driving maintenance vehicles and earth-moving machines can be hazardous. Roger Hess, who married Gerry Spike, once chased after a runaway bulldozer and prevented its likely demise by climbing aboard and reaching the controls before it headed downhill. I just recently heard about a young kid whose initials are AMR who managed to catch up with a runaway snowmobile under similar circumstances.

---

[39] See appendix

Then there was the time one summer when visitors started a fire among the pine trees on what was then Old Main Slope, now Pine Trail. Larry Weaver, Harry and Lyle's older brother, used a tractor to push highly combustible dry branches and logs out of the way so the flames could be contained before they spread up into the trees thus preventing a fire that could have spread to the rest of the area and caused serious damage. I'm not at all sure that Larry was even working for the area. In any case, he rose to the occasion. Challice recalls his face was black by the time he climbed down from the tractor.

I happened to witness this event and can't help wondering how many other deeds of this sort enabled the ski area to stay in business and continue to provide skiing for the growing number of skiers.

Appendix

Street Map of Swain in 1940s with a few corrections to Government Survey Map

1. Herthel & Alton Spencer, + children Peggy, Linda, Peter, Susie. This house had a stone mill wheel c. four feet in diameter, in center of paving for screened-in porch. (Demolished to make room for new maintenance shop.)

2. Luella & Ernie Blakley + children Ruth, Helen, Mary, Richard, Donald. Now Downhill Drew's restaurant.

3. John Brewer (owner) plus Leon and Orsina (Underwood) Spike, + children Ruth, Betty, William, Carl, Howard, Mary, Barbara, Geraldine, James, JoAnn, Thomas, Richard, Carolyn Jean, Daniel, Charles and at times Leola & Josh Underwood. (Demolished for parking.)

4. Erma Gleason Babcock's barn that became the base lodge.

5. Erma Gleason Babcock. Later Barb & Ted Swain + son Shawn. Now ski area rental property.

6. Agnes & Myrl ("Gunny") Yencer + children Marilyn, Terry, Linda. Now Agnes.

7. Margaret (Underwood) and Norman Didas + children Beverly, Mary Ellen. Later our home and ski area office. (Demolished.)

8. Mr & Mrs Livergood + children. Later Viola and Dick Blowers + children Patty, Bonnie, Jimmy, Mary Lou. Later Ski Patrol building. (Demolished.)

9. Emily ("Grandma") Dodge, later Evangelical parsonage, then ski school director Chic & Joan Carlucci. (Demolished.)

10. Anna & Ray Wirt later Marilyn (Yencer) and Lynn Weidman + children Kevin, Linsie, Amy. Now Marilyn.

11. Effie & Mel Cobin. Now converted to lodging as Mountainside Inn.

12. Maude & Fred Blakley + children Wilma, Fred Junior, store; now Challice Robinson + daughter Ariel Bailey and Maude's Country Store (pizza and sub shop in winter).

13. Lula & Ben Blakely, then Joan (Carnes) & Greg Carpenter + sons David, Craig, Sheldon. Now owned by skiers.

14. Marilyn Weidman (town historian) remembers this building as a barn.

15. Ruth & Glen Yencer + children Virginia and Gary, now Shelly & Mike Swarthout + daughter Alicia.

16. Grace & Omar Boyd + daughter Doris. Now rental property.

17. Elsie & Fred Neetz + sons Charles, Leonard. Now skiers.

18. Clyde & Howard Macomber. Now skiers.

19. Clyde Macomber. Now skiers.

20. Ruth & Rev. Frank Karr (minister and mail carrier) + children Stephen, Phillip, Vivien. Now skiers.

21. Jenny Pitcher followed by Dean and Melanie (Smith) Kingsberry. Now skiers.

22. Charlotte & Phil Hamilton. Now rental property.

23. Esther & John Harvey + children Esther, Virginia, Milton. Now skiers.

24. Joe Blakley former town hall. (Demolished)

25. Grandma Blakley, later Viola & Dick Blowers + children Patty, Bonnie. Jimmy, Mary Lou. Now Marge and Jimmy Blowers + children Jim, Jr. and Mary 2nd & 3rd generations).

26. Helen & Ken Merriman + son Dudley, grocery store. Now Sierra Restaurant and Bar.

27. Methodist Church later Marilyn & Lynn Weidman. Now rental property.

28. Gladys Newville + children Jim, Jean, Mary, Bobby. Now rental property.

29. Evangelical Church now United Methodist Church.

30. Eleanor & Robert Shoemaker + children Jimmy, Bob, Kathy, Robin, Keith. (Jimmy now has Outside Inn farther up valley.) Now Willy Cleland.

31. Joe and Leonard (Doc) Underwood. (Demolished.)

32. Marie & Eldred (Dutch) Ludwig + children Helen, Kit, Lois, Fred, Neal, Esther. Original post office, later home of Esther (nee Ludwig) & John Dieter + children Michael and Karen. Now home of 3rd and 4th generations: Debby & Michael Dieter + children Aaron, Angela, Amy.

33. Nora Mess. (Demolished.)

34. Julia & Lawrence Weaver + sons Larry, Harry, Lyle. (Demolished.)

35. Anna & Delbert France + children Art, Dale, Dorothy. (Demolished.)

36. Marion & Clare Macomber. Later Norma and Phil Isaman + children Arlen, Phyllis, Shirley. (Demolished.)

37. Ruth & Carl Sleight + children John, Cheryl, Brenda. (Demolished.)

38. Rosamond & Sydney May + sons Gerald, Charles (Chuck). (Demolished.)

39. Rosetta & Del Delaney. (Demolished.)

40. Carl & Pearl Underwood + daughters Marie, Gwennie. Now skiers.

41. Dolly & Rudy Underwood + children LaRue (Butch), Cheryl, Michael. Now (daughter) Cheryl and Randy Burros.

42. Lula & Leo Griffith + son Burton. Now Jesse Griffith, 3rd generation

43. Mary & Charles May + children Steven, Mitchell, Brian, Michelle. Now skiers who are also full-time residents Robin and Jim Raffa.

44. Gertrude ("Gertie") Wood, long-time town clerk, followed by Julia & Lawrence Weaver + sons Larry, Harry, Lyle. Now Harry's son Cory, 3rd generation.

45. Lillian & Kenneth Carnes + daughters Barbara, Sandra, Joan, Dianne, Nancy. Now skiers.

46. Eunice and Lester Gaby + children Dean, Jean, Roger, Keith. Now skiers.

47. Dolores & Hugh Swain + children Ronald, Gary, Jeanine, Gregory, Rodney. Dolores remains.

Of the 45 houses (Two of the 47 on the list were barns.) standing in the 1940's, 14 have been demolished primarily due to the ski area. Of the remaining 31 houses, 19 are either rental properties or part-time residences of skiers compared to 12 that remain the full-time residence of their owners. There are six new full-time residences, 16 condos, six chalets, and two apartments (converted from former four-unit motel).

These houses are all within the hamlet itself and do not take into account the numerous cabins and homes built farther up Ewart Creek, along Swain Hill Road and the colony of chalets on the Whitney farm overlooking the ski area. The number of full-time residents has shrunk from 120 to 40, however, partly due to families having fewer children as well as the reduction in full-time residents.

Footnote 39 – from last page of book.

Dolores and Dorine were the daughters of Rose and Bob Klossner. Bob was a Swiss immigrant, but he must have come over at a young age as he had no accent. They maintained a long pond in the valley along what is now Route 70 and a lodge where fishers and hunters could stay in addition to farming the fields that remained on the side of the valley above the pond. One of their crops was apples from an old orchard. Bob was well-known in the area for the excellent hard cider he produced from these apples.

Bob once presented me with a large rock weighing well over 100 pounds. I have no idea how he knew I would like it, but I did. He was not a very large man, not much taller than my 5'4", but strong. A smooth rock like that one with nothing to get a grip on, is much harder to carry than an object with something to get grip on. I was amazed how he carried it from his truck, across the front of the base lodge and deposited on the spot I had designated in a flower bed near our house and office without realizing he was going to just pick it up and carry it. That rock now rests outside our present house because we brought it with us after we retired and moved to the other side of the hill on land bought from Gertrude and Clarence Nichols.

INDEX

A

Adams, Adam 199
Aitchison, Thomas Cant 141
Aitchison, Winifred Maude Binless 142
Auntie Betty 90, 186. *See* Bruggeman, Elizabeth
Aunt Nell 2, 4, 18, 24, 144, 170. *See* Robinson, Eleanor
Austin, Glenn 101, 200

B

Babcock, Erma Gleason 7, 20, 27, 46, 153, 215
Baker, Hollis 81, 112
Baker, Steve, Buzzy, Moe, Bill, Shelia 112
Baker, Vivian 85, 86, 112
Bank of Castile, The 10, 83, 144, 147, 189
Base Lodge 7, 9, 77, 126, 127
Blades, Lee and Bob 33
Blakley, Ben 20, 48, 55, 72, 160
Blakley, Dolores 115, 213
Blakley, Ernie 32, 156, 215
Blakley, Fred and Maude 6, 7, 9, 32, 33, 35, 54, 63, 72, 125, 144, 154, 157, 165, 216
Blakley, Junior 32
Blakley, Susie 89
Blowers, Dick and Viola 62, 63, 99, 178, 215, 217
Blowers, Jimmy 99, 163, 217
Blowers, Patty, Bonnie, Mary Lou 99
Bombardier 38, 39, 194, 198
Bousquet's Ski Center 2, 3, 17, 61, 109, 134
Brewer, John 7, 20, 27, 41, 53, 98, 215
Bristol Hills 3, 4, 17, 104
Brockport Central School 7, 17
Brown, Ernie 200

Bruggeman, Elizabeth Aitchison ix. *See* Auntie Betty
Bunker 37
Burby Hollow 3, 17, 53
Butler, Don 197

C

Cafeteria Crew, The 85
Canandaigua Lake 2, 4, 18, 19, 24, 170, 199
Canaseraga 6, 29, 33, 41, 46, 48, 54, 74, 79, 85, 86, 105, 111, 117, 151, 153–155, 161–168, 187, 208, 209
Canaseraga Creek 54, 74, 153, 155, 161–163, 168
Carlucci, Brian and Karen 106, 188
Carlucci, Chic and Joan ix, 104–107, 116, 165, 188, 216
Carnes, Barbara, Sandra, Joan, Dianne and Nancy 160
Carnes, Lillian and Kenneth 158–160, 218
Carpenter, David, Craig, Sheldon 160
Carpenter, Joanne and Greg 86, 94, 216
Champion, Cliff 97, 199
Christie 37, 38
Clark, David, Dianne, Bill and Gail 25
Clark, Dick 6, 8, 25, 39, 43, 47, 77, 97, 98, 101
Clark, Mary 8, 9, 85, 89
Cleland, Calvin 197
Cobin, Effie and Mel 155, 157, 216
Coombs, Bob, Marty, Fran, Phil, and Ray 30
Coombs, Gail and Winnie 29
Crawford, Teresa and Jim 156
Cromwell, Mildred 44
Cubberly, Mitch 114, 122
Cubco 114

D

Dalton Phone Company 44
Depression, The Great 141
DeWolfe, Bill 17, 103, 110
DeWolfe, Helen 175

Dieter, Esther and John 86, 94, 158, 217
Dieter, Karen and Michael 217
Dresser, Cleve 79

E

Eastman Kodak 5, 15
Edwards, Charlie 97
Ellicottville 9, 17, 53
Emerson, Marian, M.D. and George, M.D. 99
Ewart Creek 21, 48, 54, 74, 160, 161, 166, 219

F

France, Anna and Del 36
France, Arthur, Dorothy and Dale 37
French toast 92, 146

G

Gaby, Eunice 88, 111, 119, 131, 154, 158, 183
General Electric vii, 15, 142
Griffith, Lula 86, 145, 203

H

Halbert, Marty 187
Hall, Vic 47, 64
Haller, Mrs. 16
Hamlet of Swain vii, viii, 13, 41, 151, 164, 166
Harder, Allan, M.D. 52, 99
Harder, Betty, M.D. 99
Harley School 8, 31
Hausman, John and Betsy 164, 167
Heath, Mark 20, 52, 153
Hedden, Dave 112, 115
Hess, Roger 198, 213
Hill, Dwight 97

Holiday Valley 9, 17
Hurni, Max 122
Hurricane Agnes 161–163

I

Isaman, Phil and Norma 46, 195, 218

J

James, Bob 74
James, Matthew and Bethany (daughter Janet's children) 204
Jenkins, Bill 10, 93, 133, 138, 196, 213
Jenkins, Dorine 213, 219
Johnson, Donny 112, 210
Johnson, Terry 115, 135

K

Kelly, Walt 44
Kendall, Dorothy ix
Kerr, Hilda and Harold 156
Kester, Gordy 4
Killy 136, 178, 204
King, Floyd 35, 67, 121
Kingsbury, Dean and Melanie 181
Kingston, Ross 163
Kissing Bridge Ski Center 10
Kitt, AJ 107, 189
Kitt, Nancy and Ross 107, 189
Klein, Mike 2
Klipnocky District School 88
Klos, Grace 85
Knights, Harry 144, 208
Kodak, Eastman Kodak 5, 15
Kreiley, Charlie 33, 48
Kron, Marty 97, 199

L

Lake Erie 4, 20
Lake Ontario 4
Lapham, Glenn 105, 187
Lehman, Herb ix
Livingston, Jerry 168
Livingston, Joanne 117
Long, Dave and Joey 115
Ludwig, Kit, Helen, Lois, Neal and Esther 158
Ludwig, Marie and Eldred ("Dutch") 158

M

Maul, Dave (Heavy) 132, 194
May, Chuck 162, 165
May, Mary and Chuck 165
May, Steven, Mitchell, and twins Michelle and Brian 165
McFarland, Jim M.D. 99
McHenry, Ethel 13
Merriman, Helen and Ken 156, 217
Metivier, Don 11
Meyering, Ray 47, 97, 199
Miller, Bob and Lu 107
Miller, Earl 114, 122
Miller, Judy, Tom, Kris, Dave and Andrea 107, 181
Moffatt, Ken 188
Morsch, Art 86
Murphy, Bill 97
Muxworthy, Gary 120
Muxworthy's Ski Loft 120
Myers, Nate 112

N

Neary, Del 86, 181
Neetz, Elsie and Fred 163
Newmark, Bernie 47, 70
Newville, Gladys 163, 217
Nichols, Clarence 181, 219

O

Old Forge 17, 140

P

Panogataga, Steve (Wegman's) 94
Paris Hotel 120
Petrick, Tim 106
Philadelphia vii, 2, 3, 13–17
Pierce, Bill 33, 48, 81, 112
Pierce, Bummy 81, 112
Pierce, Dennis 112
Pierce, Leila 86
Pittsfield 2, 3, 15, 17, 61
Plumb, Ralph 103
Powdermill Park 17
Pownall, Jenny and Jamie (daughter Jeanie's children) 190
Pownall, Jim ix, 137, 189
Pyranol 15

R

Rawleigh, Danny ("Moon") 112
Redfield, George 156
Robinson, Alice Mae (Challice) 18, 144
Robinson, Andrew McLeod ix, 191
Robinson, Ariel (daughter Challice's child) 172, 174
Robinson, Challice Binless ix, 173
Robinson, David and Colin (son Andy's twin sons) 156
Robinson, Eleanor Davison 24. *See* Aunt Nell
Robinson, Janet Davison ix, 201
Robinson, Ray McLeod 18, 144
Robinson-Pownall, Jean (Jeanie) Aitchison ix, 183
Rochester 2, 3, 5, 14, 15, 17, 18, 20, 29, 31, 32, 35, 38, 44, 52, 53, 67, 70, 75, 76, 85, 97, 99, 103, 104, 106, 121, 141, 143, 148, 167, 181, 231
Roffe, Diann 106

S

Sanford, Rick 117
Saunders, Bonnie 86
Sawmill 32, 35, 41, 56, 78, 79, 160
Schiavetti, Nick viii, ix
Schmidtman, Werner 199
Schobinger, Charles 2
Scott, Joe 81, 173, 180, 202
Seitz, Don 97
Sherman, John and Judy 199
Ski Patrol, Swain viii, ix, 1, 8, 25, 97, 101
Ski School, Swain 103, 122
Ski Shop, Swain 109
Smith, Robin 11, 65, 84, 104, 116, 122, 149, 185, 189
Smith, Ruth 86
Smith, Terry 98
Snowmaking 4, 9, 10, 23, 24, 50, 67, 69, 73, 75, 76, 78, 110, 148, 149, 180, 184, 197
Snow Ridge 17
Spencer, Alton 54, 110, 215
Spencer, Dena 117
Spike, Gerry 200, 213
Spike, Ky 181
Spike, Orsina ("Siney") and Leon 27, 146, 181
Spike, Ruth, Betty, William, Carl, Howard, Mary, Barbara, Geraldine, James, JoAnn, Thomas, Richard, Carolyn Jean, Daniel, Charles 27, 215
Stevens, Bob 176
Stoneham, Harry ix, 98, 101, 200
Swain, Barb and Ted 46, 87, 125, 186, 195, 203
Swain, Dave 40
Swain, Dolores and Hugh 155
Swain, Duane ("Buster") 37, 112
Swain, Hamlet of vii, viii, 13, 41, 151, 164, 166
Swain, Ronald, Gary, Jeanine, Rodney, and Gregory 155
Swain, Samuel 151
Swain, Shawn 46, 187, 215

Swain Rental Department 52, 74, 84, 89, 112
Swain Ski School 103, 122
Swain Ski Shop and Rental Department 109
Szabo, Irene 155

T

Tardiff, Dick 8, 97
Taylor, Ed 9, 54
Thiokol 40, 197
Tows and Lifts 59
Tucker, Beverly 89, 95
Tucker, Lucille 86, 90, 94, 175, 186
Tucker, Paul, Kevin and Karen 94, 175
Tucker SnoCats 199

U

Underwood, Carl 32, 35, 63
Underwood, Gwennie 183
Underwood, LaRue ("Butch") 112
University of Rochester 2, 14, 231

V

VanArsdale, Bud 10, 83, 147
Vine Valley 2, 4

W

Wadsworth, Bill 45
Wagenblass, David "Wheels" 187
Weaver, Harry ix, 37–40, 56, 65, 110, 133, 193–198, 212, 214
Weaver, Larry 214
Weaver, Lyle ix, 133, 193, 196–199, 212, 214
Wegman's Food Markets 94
Weidman, Kevin, Linsie and Amy 28

Weidman, Marilyn and Lynn 27, 28, 33, 40, 47, 166, 168, 187, 216, 217
Whitney, Bill 21, 53, 156
Whitney, Mary, Helen, Judy and Nellie 167
Wirt, Anna and Ray 27
Wirt, LaVerne and Jean 81, 89, 202
Wirt, Mike 131
Woodstock, VT 59
World War II vii, 98, 104, 118, 120, 154, 231

Y

Yencer, Agnes and Gunny 33, 45, 47, 48, 65, 69, 82, 145, 154, 161, 166
Yole, Al 97
Young, Wende M.D. 75

About the Authors

Caught up in the demands of World War II, newlyweds Dave and Bina Robinson planned for the years ahead when they would be able to pursue their own destiny instead of responding to the demands of the war. The result was the creation of a ski area involving decades of hard work while holding down other full-time jobs to pay the bills. Sixty years later, as octogenarians, they have written the true story of their endeavors and experiences of this remarkable undertaking.

Avid hikers, they joined the British Ramblers Association for two treks in Nepal, one a 30-day circuit of Anna Purna led by Sherpas and assisted by porters. Other excursions included trips to the Dolomites, Peru, Andorra and numerous rambles in the English Lake District and the American southwest.

Both are life-long writers. Bina was the sports editor of "The Tower Times," the student newspaper of the women's campus at their alma mater, the University of Rochester, and Dave was a contributor to the men's paper "The Campus." After retiring, Dave became a regular contributor to "The Finger Lakes Review," an historical journal; and a contributing editor to "The New England Journal of Antiquities," an anthropological journal. The advent of the word processor aided in his very active decades-long correspondence with numerous friends with long letters that more than one recipient considered worth collecting for posterity. Bina is best known for her dedicated work and editorials on animal & human welfare, human health, and environmental issues, and her webpage on the same (www.linkny.com/~civitas). She served as a local correspondent and feature writer for "The Hornell Evening Tribune" and had numerous articles and editorials published in American and British magazines before pausing to write "With Our Own Four Hands."

Printed in the United States
115626LV00004B/167/A